# AFTERMATH OF JENNIFER KESSE'S ABDUCTION

# AFTERMATH OF JENNIFER KESSE'S ABDUCTION

## An Uncle's Quest for Understanding & Inspiring Life Lessons

### Bill Gilmour

NEW DEGREE PRESS

COPYRIGHT © 2023 BILL GILMOUR

AFTERMATH OF JENNIFER KESSE'S ABDUCTION
*An Uncle's Quest for Understanding & Inspiring Life Lessons*

ISBN

979-8-88504-440-0   *Paperback*
979-8-88504-463-9   *Digital Ebook*

To Jennifer—know you are loved. We have never given up hope and continue to pray for answers.

To Joyce, Drew, and Logan—you are loved. Despite the enormous pain you carry, your love for Jenn and pursuit of justice for her and others are inspiring.

Evil will not have the last word.

# CONTENTS

# INTRODUCTION

*When suffering happens, it forces us to confront*
*life in a different way than we normally do.*

—PHILIP YANCEY

 Jennifer was missing. She hadn't shown up for work, her car was gone, and all calls from family, friends, and coworkers went directly to voicemail.

Tuesday, January 24, 2006, is a day my family will never forget.

My sister Joyce called me early that morning; unfortunately, I was on an airplane traveling to a much colder New Jersey on business. We played telephone tag until around 6 p.m. that evening. When we finally connected, Joyce's voice sounded different: a combination of fear and deep concern. I knew something serious and unexpected had happened.

Joyce told me that my niece Jennifer was missing.

Two days later, we learned she had been abducted. Jennifer's abduction changed every family member's life forever. We went from watching news stories to being the news story. We went from a momentary sense of sadness and concern to profound anguish, helplessness, and hopelessness. Every January 24 serves as a painful reminder of that Tuesday in 2006.

While writing this book, the world has been immersed in the global COVID-19 pandemic, impacting every person in some way. Those who have contracted this potentially life-threatening virus suffer from various symptoms, some long-lasting, while many others have lost their lives.

We continue to experience fear, anxiety, and uncertainty in the aftermath of masking and mandated requirements of physical distancing and social isolation from family, friends, and workplaces.

Zoom and other video conferencing tools have eased the pain and impact as we quickly transitioned work meetings to the virtual environment. An additional benefit was scheduling "virtual" gatherings with family and friends. However, as the weeks and months dragged on, we realized the importance of being physically present and personally involved with the people in our lives. We longed for the opportunity to hold, hug, or be in the company of others to share life.

Negative news seems never-ending. Skimming headlines, we move from economic and political challenges at home, to the Russian war in Ukraine, and the humanitarian, economic, and global geopolitical ramifications. Amid all this, we marked the twenty-first anniversary of the 9/11 attack on the United States. Every 9/11 anniversary is personal to me because a good friend's son died at work in One World Trade Center.

Significant events in human history: global—war, natural disasters, famine, pandemics—or personal—illness, job loss, financial, physical, and relational challenges—or death bring about fear and anxiety as well as pain and suffering. Amid these circumstances, we desire hope. We long to have a sense of peace and a return to better times.

Hope is a universal aspiration, a word we all use and desire. Yet, how often have you said to someone, "I hope that works out for you," or I "hope so" in response to a conversation with someone? But what is hope? How does the world or culture define hope?

The online version of *Merriam-Webster's Dictionary* offers the following components of hope: to want something to happen or be true; hope for a promotion; hoping for the best (MERRIAM-WEBSTER).

In other words, a wishful hoping, the "I-hope-that-works-out-for-you" kind of hope. Have you discovered *Webster's 1828 Dictionary*? If not, I highly recommend looking up commonly used words today to see how they were defined generations ago. For example, how does Webster's 1828 dictionary define hope? First, this version has an expectation of confidence for hope. Importantly for our journey together, *Webster's 1828 Dictionary* says hope includes:

- Confidence in a future event;
- The highest degree of well-founded expectation of good;
- A *hope founded on God's gracious promises.*

Finally, the dictionary defines hope as an opinion or belief not amounting to certainty but grounded on *substantial evidence* (WEBSTER'S DICTIONARY 1828).

My goal in writing this book is to *inspire hope* by sharing my life experiences authentically. To vulnerably share the sorrow, fear, trials, and temptations, along with breakthrough moments that provided encouragement and hope. In the personal stories included, we learn we all have relatable shared experiences as we live out our seventy-plus years on earth. Through them, we can discover who we are and in whom we receive hope.

*Inspired hope* is not wishful thinking; rather, it is a confident expectation only found in one person through an intimate relationship that lasts our lifetime.

Pastor and author Andy Stanley declared, "When somebody predicts their own death and resurrection and pulls it off, we should go with whatever that person says" (Stanley 2018). I agree. The only person to ever predict their death and resurrection was Jesus of Nazareth. So, the *inspired hope* I am talking about is not a "hope-so" or "I-hope-that-works-out-for-you" kind of wishful thinking. It is a hope *know*—a hope with certainty. A *confident* hope built upon evidence and documented eyewitness accounts.

*John, an early follower of Jesus, authored several documents in our present-day Bibles. In the Gospel of John, his big takeaway was, "Jesus did many other miraculous signs in the presence of his followers which are not recorded in this book. But these are written so that you may believe that Jesus is the Christ, the Son of God. Then by believing, you may have life through His name" (JOHN 20:30–31, NCV).*

The hope I'm sharing *is* anchored to a person and a promise. The person is Jesus. The promise is that if you believe in Jesus, you *will* have life—an impactful and meaningful life. How will this happen? As John tells us, it begins with believing that Jesus is who He claimed to be: God. When we declare that truth, He rescues, redeems, and restores you and me to a right relationship with Himself. Then, amazingly, the new you will positively impact all the relationships in your life.

In the following pages, I share my journey, beginning by confronting the brutal facts about my life under circumstances I would never have chosen. However, I remain eternally grateful to have come through them with a healthier perspective. I now have peace and joy that are not dependent on my circumstances. Next, you will read about individuals who have experienced observable life transformation through extraordinary trials and testing. Their personal stories have impacted many people. The ripple effect of hope is priceless.

Importantly, from the beginning of our time together, I would like each of us to agree that we will not get caught up in the comparison game. By that, I mean we will choose not to minimize or maximize our pain, suffering, or struggles by comparing our experiences with those of others. While our trials, struggles, and challenges may share common elements with others, we will agree that each of us has to walk in and through our own circumstances. But not alone!

In a 2020 article titled "Comparative Suffering is Dangerous," Sara Buxton wrote, "Comparative suffering is a defense mechanism. And if we know anything about defense mechanisms, we know that they are only so good for so long. Comparative suffering can walk us right into resentment, bitterness and feeling burnt out" (Buxton 2020).

Sara points out that comparative suffering can lead people to become judgmental about the suffering of others. She referenced a scenario we all have had. A family member, friend, or neighbor calls you to complain about their salary cut. You listen, roll your eyes, and think, *I've lost my job. I'm still unemployed, and you're complaining, really!* First, each of us must process what we feel in our circumstances. Then, filtered through our personal life experiences, we seek to find and offer compassion.

The road ahead will include some rocky paths, slippery slopes, and uncomfortable terrain that is our current lives and relationships. As you pursue a new you, your preferred future, some people in your life will not be happy. They may think you are just in a phase or your next fad, and your changed behavior won't last. Some may wait for you to stumble and fall so they can say, "See? We knew this wasn't real; you're the same old person." However, most people in your life will encourage and cheer you on to finish strong. I'll be in that crowd!

All of this may sound good, but as the adage reminds us, it is easier said than done. We will discover this is a quest taken one step at a time. Some days, we will take a few steps backward, and that's okay! Our adventure together will be long and challenging as we confront years of habits, hang-ups, and hurt, along with our misguided and misinformed decisions.

*You are only one defining decision away*
*from a totally different life!*
—MARK BATTERSON (BATTERSON 2013, 18)

Looking back, I am grateful for making that defining decision to change the narrative direction of my life. I believe my family would agree. What was the decision I made? I chose to start with myself first. I intentionally decided to become the person I wished other people would be. The result? My attitudes, actions, and words changed, and the people in my life realized that life transformation is possible. Old dogs *can* change!

As we travel on this great adventure together, relish the time on the mountaintops celebrating the triumphs while appreciating incredible vistas of hope. Then, in the valleys, when the journey gets tough and the terrain challenging, take a moment to reflect and journal what you've learned. You're on a quest worth the risks and challenges you will encounter.

Let's begin by reigniting our dreams and aspirations buried under piles of life's struggles. Believe in yourself and know you have a God who believes in you, even if you don't believe in Him. He knows your name and is cheering you on.

Imagine a day when you share your story of finding hope with the people in your life. Your persistence, patience, and perseverance will inspire and encourage them and future generations to become better versions of themselves.

My prayer for every person reading this book is that you *will* begin your journey of life transformation. You will not settle for the status quo, the easy, or the expected. Instead, you will recognize a deep desire that there is more to this life and more to you. Notably, you will meet hope amid your pain and suffering, trials, and tests. You will experience peace, joy, and gratitude in your current circumstances. And yes, I did say peace, joy, and gratitude *in* your circumstances, especially the challenging ones.

May each of us confidently say, "I know without a doubt that the present me is better than the past me, and I look forward to the future me!"

Are you up for the journey? Are you the person you want to be? Are you ready to take the first step?

PART ONE

# AN UNRAVELING LIFE

CHAPTER 1

# JENNIFER IS MISSING

*What we must not do is surrender to despair and hopelessness*
*and the cynical assumption that there is nothing we can do.*
*What we must do is turn our anger and outrage into a positive*
*force for reforms that can help prevent future tragedies.*

—BERNICE KING

When you live in Florida, you quickly learn bodies of water are everywhere. According to the Fish and Wildlife Conservation Commission, "There are more than 7,500 lakes, ponds, and reservoirs, and approximately 12,000 miles of fishable rivers, streams, and canals" (Fish and Wildlife Commission). Many of these ponds, lakes, and canals are along roadways.

And what lives in those bodies of water? Alligators. Locals warned us to be careful walking near water, especially with pets or small children. Alligators move very fast in or out of water. According to the Key West Aquarium website, Florida is home to over one million alligators (Aquarium 2022).

It was common in Florida to hear about a car that veered off the road and submerged in water, only to be found days or weeks later when water levels dropped enough for a part of the car to be visible. Where was Jenn's car? Did she end up in a canal?

After the call with Joyce that Tuesday evening, I kept replaying our conversation. Jennifer was missing, and I felt utterly helpless to do anything about it. That night, I spoke with my business partners, explained what had happened, and made plans to fly back to Orlando the next day.

As I tried to sleep, my mind played out all the possible dark scenarios of what could have happened to Jenn. Then, my mind drifted to making mental lists of things to do. How would we search all the bodies of water on Jenn's route to work?

Nothing made sense. Jenn was living her dream. She purchased her first home—a condominium at Mosaic at Millenia in Orlando in the fall of 2005—and a new car, a black 2006 Chevrolet Malibu. Jenn was on a great career path and was excelling in her position. And she had someone she cared about in her life, Rob Allen.

As Joyce described Jenn: "Those of us close to Jenn, we knew something must be wrong. If she was going to be late for work or a meeting, she would call. In fact, Jenn had good routines. She and Rob, her boyfriend, called each other daily while driving to work in the morning and would speak with each other every night before going to bed."

Joyce told me, "Drew and I talked with Jenn last night [Monday evening]. Jenn mentioned that she had already spoken with Rob." We later learned from Rob that he had an early morning meeting (Tuesday, January 24, 2006), so he and Jenn couldn't talk during her drive to work. Instead, he said he'd call after the meeting.

Joyce and Drew were close friends with Tom, a senior executive with Central Florida Investments, Jenn's employer. When Tom learned that Jenn did not show up for work, he called them to see if they had heard from her. They immediately started calling Jenn's cell and home numbers without success. Internal alarms were going off.

What we knew at that time was whatever happened was totally out of character for Jennifer. She was predictable in a good way. She was intelligent, always conscious of her surroundings, and planned for her safety. For example, Joyce said when Jenn was leaving the mall, a restaurant, or a meeting in the evening, she would call someone and talk until she was safely in her car.

Those who knew Jennifer would agree she didn't show any signs of discontent with her life, relationships, or work environment.

However, I learned Jenn had some uncomfortable experiences with some workers at her condo complex. Anyone who has bought a new home knows there will be continuing involvement with the developer and maintenance staff for some time. Unfortunately, Jenn lived alone and felt like she was being watched and subjected to unwelcome stares.

Jenn shared her concerns with her father. As a result, Drew told her to call if she ever felt threatened or in danger, and he would come to Orlando and take care of it. She also made a formal complaint to the property management company. Based on Jenn's concerns, Joyce and Drew immediately suspected the workers when they realized Jenn was missing.

**ABDUCTED**

SINCE JAN. 24, 2006 ORLANDO, FL

**Name:** Jennifer Kesse
**Age:** 24
**Description:** 5'8" Shoulder
Length Sandy Blonde Hair, Green
Eyes, 125lbs

**$REWARD$**

WWW.FindJenniferKesse.com

Call a lawyer or
**321-235-5300**       **1-800-423-TIPS**
Orlando Police              Crime Line

By the time I arrived at Jenn's condo on January 25, Drew already had missing-person flyers printed. Family and friends began to canvass the buildings in her complex and local neighborhoods, handing out flyers and looking for Jenn's car.

Eventually, many of us went to the main road intersections. We handed out flyers to people as they waited in their cars for the lights to change.

Debbie and I visited the local businesses and shopping centers near Jenn's condo, asking permission to tape the flyers to doors and windows and leaving some on counters. While this was important, a little part of me felt like we needed to be doing more. *I* needed to be doing more.

On the evening of Wednesday, January 25, as we gathered at Jenn's condo, I felt the need to be busy doing something. First, we needed to find Jenn's car. I had been involved with several political campaigns and was familiar with planning door-to-door activities. In my mind, if we did a street-by-street search for Jenn's car, it might lead us to Jenn. So, we organized groups and assigned specific streets to canvass.

For a moment, I felt hopeful. By midnight, my wife Debbie, my sister Marge, and I finished for the night in a neighborhood at the southwest corner of Americana Boulevard and Texas Avenue in Orlando, just a mile from Jenn's condo.

The following day, Thursday, January 26, we gathered at Jenn's condo to organize and send groups out to continue our street search.

Drew's phone rang. "Hello, this is Drew Kesse," he answered, turning solemnly as he made eye contact with Joyce and everyone present. Our eyes were staring expectantly at him, waiting.

My heart raced with anticipation. Seconds felt like hours.

Drew hit the end button on his phone and, in a quiet voice, said, "It was the Orlando Police. They said there was a break in the case. They found Jenn's car."

Almost simultaneously, those present said, "Where?"

"A resident at the Huntington on the Green apartments called the OPD tip line after seeing Jenn's car on the news," Drew told us. "Police confirmed it was Jennifer's black 2006 Chevy Malibu."

*Huntington on the Green? We were across the street last night.*
Almost immediately, Debbie, my sister Marge, and I looked at each other in disbelief. We all had a sinking, nauseous feeling; we had just been in that neighborhood the night before, looking for Jenn's car.

With her car found, local media outlets arrived at her condo community, along with law enforcement agencies. Helicopters began flying overhead, and before long, K-9 units arrived to start a search of the area. Within days, Terry, a neighbor from Lake Mary and an officer with the Mounted Unit of Orange County Sheriff's department, had organized a search of off-road and wooded areas.

Our collective faces revealed growing concern and increasing anxiety. They have Jenn's car, but where is Jenn? Emotions were high as we tried to make sense of what was happening. Time seemed to have painfully stopped.

I was amazed at how Drew was handling the situation. Early in our marriages, we lived on the same cul-de-sac in Barnegat, New Jersey. Drew was an accomplished sales professional. He had a remarkable ability to persevere despite being told "no" dozens of times a day while cold calling for business. He seemed to thrive in that environment. Drew's family was his top priority, and he would do anything to protect them. But now, he was thrust into one of the most challenging situations any parent could face: having a missing child.

Drew was the point person with law enforcement and the media while seeking to calm everyone with confidence that belied the situation and his internal emotions. His determination and focus encouraged all of us. One night, we stood outside Jenn's condo in the interior breezeway and talked.

The tone of his voice and body language revealed the overwhelming stress he was experiencing.

"What are you thinking? What do you want us to do next?" I asked.

Drew's face and quietness revealed he was reflecting on the enormity of the situation.

"Drew, I want you to know how proud I am of you. How proud we all are," I said encouragingly. "I can't imagine what you are carrying right now." Then, after a pause, I continued, "I have always been amazed by your professionalism, tenacity, and persistence. You will draw on the confidence and courage you have displayed in life and work." With my eyes fixed on his, I extended my right arm to his shoulder. "You don't know what you're capable of doing until you have to do it. You *will* do it—and you have family and friends here to support you."

Drew got us all focused on promoting awareness. We knew how important it was to tell people that Jenn was missing and show a picture of her and then one of her car, hoping someone would remember seeing something.

Within a few days, we learned the Huntington on the Green apartment complex had security cameras. Police reviewed the video footage, and though the quality was not good, it was clear someone other than Jenn drove her car to that location, parked it, and then walked away. So now, a person of interest needed to be located and identified. Two people needed to be found.

We faced a new reality: Jennifer had been abducted. Our priority to get her story in front of the public increased dramatically. We needed anyone with information to step up and share what they might know with the authorities.

Emotions were all over the map—glad for new information, yet overwhelmed with a sense of loss and grief, sorrow, and sadness. What happened to Jenn, and where was she?

Jenn's story received excellent news coverage across central Florida and beyond. The details of the search for Jennifer and the investigation continue to this day. Drew ensures her story remains on news programs, podcasts, articles, and websites.

But the question we all asked and wondered was, how—and why—does someone vanish without a trace?

And that question ignited a flood of personal questions that began to pierce my heart and soul.

## CHAPTER 2

# MY LIFE IS UNRAVELING

*A man who lies to himself, and believes his own lies becomes unable to recognize truth, either in himself or in anyone else, and he ends up losing respect for himself and for others.*

—FYODOR DOSTOEVSKY

During the day, our family and friends were constantly amazed and encouraged by everyone who would come to help us find Jenn. Thinking about it now is still emotional. People came together in the community to help a family in need, a family they didn't know. Jennifer's story reminded us that we are all someone's daughter or son. None of us could fully grasp the weight of emotions my sister, brother-in-law, and nephew carried. But we could come alongside them and support and encourage them by showing up.

Every night, I was exhausted, lying in bed, trying to fall asleep. But I couldn't turn my mind off. I tried to make sense of what had happened to Jennifer, but how do you make sense of something so senseless? And then I thought about my marriage, business, and kids. Most nights were filled with tears, as my emotions were in hyperdrive, trying to process everything I was experiencing.

Every night was restless. I felt vulnerable, completely exposed. It was as if I was in a continual wrestling match with my past. I recalled my actions, attitudes, and words from many experiences and encounters with people. And I seemed to be on the losing end of each match. Every night, the brutal facts of my present reality hit me as if I were in a sparring match with a boxer. Facing reality was—and still is—painful, but I would learn it can also be beneficial and transformative if embraced.

> *Vulnerability 'softens' people and opens*
> *them up to the possibility of change.*
>
> —JOHN MATTONE (MATTONE 2020, 42)

I began crying out to God, which was puzzling since I had walked away from the Church when I was fourteen. My early church memories were more like a nightmare. The teaching focused on using fear to correct behavior. If I didn't behave right, wasn't "good," didn't go to confession, and go to church every week, then God, acting as a judge, would *get* me. God was up in heaven, distant, not directly involved in my life, watching me and waiting for me to screw up. And when I did, He would punish me somehow, some way. Even then, I remember thinking, *This didn't make any sense.*

Fear was the common theme. At no time was having a personal relationship with God ever discussed. I don't recall opening a Bible or being encouraged to read one. I *do* remember being hit in the back of the head with a Bible because I was talking in church one Sunday morning.

After all those years of bad teaching, I still believed in God—just not the God that had been described to me. So I walked away from the Church. No, I ran away as fast as possible.

But now, I was facing the most desperate and challenging crisis in my life, with nowhere to go and no one to turn to—but God. On those tear-filled nights, I began having conversations with God. I desperately wanted to believe He had heard me. And more importantly, He cared about me and what happened to Jenn. How would He respond? How would I know?

Pain, helplessness, and hopelessness brought me to the point at which I would do almost anything for relief, answers, help, or hope. C.S. Lewis wrote,

God whispers to us in our pleasures, speaks in our conscience, but shouts in our pains: it is His megaphone to rouse a deaf world (Lewis 2011).

Relief came as I released the burdens carried on my shoulders to God in those nightly conversations. Whew! All that weight was taken away—simply by sharing my heart and soul. I talked with Him as if He was one of my best friends. For the first time in my life, I acknowledged I wasn't in control and was, in fact, powerless over the current situation. I admitted to God I had made a mess of my life.

## OUR HOPES AND DREAMS FALL APART

The hard truth was, in the last months of 2005, at night, Debbie and I would hold tightly to our sides of the mattress to avoid touching each other. Looking back, I recognize how sad and pathetic it was. And worse, I did nothing about it. After Jennifer went missing, Debbie confided that she hadn't been wearing her engagement or wedding rings for more than a month. Teary-eyed, I never even noticed. So how did we get to this point? How did I get to this place?

Debbie and I met in September 1979 through mutual friends. My neighbor Sandy was close friends with Kathy, a registered nurse who worked with Debbie. Sandy suggested hosting us at her home so Debbie and I would be comfortable for our "blind date." Seeing Debbie for the first time left me speechless. I know many guys say that, but anyone who knows me knows I am a talker and never at a loss for words. But that night, something—no, someone, Debbie—had caused me to be quiet.

From that first night, we spent some time together every day. We enjoyed being with each other. Over time, we knew we would get married. We shared our hopes and dreams and began discussing what our lives would be like in the future. We made plans, and we had good intentions. But looking back, how did we end up drifting so far apart? How did I allow our relationship to stray from those hopes and dreams we shared in the early years?

November 1, 2005, was our twenty-fifth wedding anniversary. However, as the year ended, our relationship deteriorated rapidly. On a drive from New Jersey to Richmond, Virginia, with one of my business partners, Alan, I was talking to Debbie on the phone. Alan couldn't help but hear the loud conversation. So, he and I had our first honest, personal conversation. Over the next five hours, we learned more about each other.

After a pause in our conversation, Alan asked me a question I've never forgotten: "What do you think 2006 is going to look like based on your current situation?"

I didn't respond immediately. Facing reality can do that. With my head down and a low voice, "We're probably going to get divorced."

Alan then shared that his first marriage ended in divorce. I was fourteen when my parents separated and divorced. It was not a pleasant experience for anyone. When I married

Debbie, I intended to stay married. Yet, despite my best intentions, divorce was a real possibility. In addition to my marriage, the business I started was struggling. The wheels were starting to fall off, and my life would soon be careening out of control.

## HELPFUL INFORMATION

In 2008, I read *The Principle of the Path: How to Get from Where You Are to Where You Want to Be*. Andy Stanley wrote something that resonated with me:

> *Direction—not intention—determines our destination. The direction you are currently traveling—relationally, financially, spiritually, and the list goes on—will determine where you end up on each of those respective arenas. This is true regardless of your goals, your dreams, your wishes or your wants…And like every principle, you can leverage this one to your advantage or ignore it to your disadvantage. Just as there are paths that have led us to places we never intended to be, there are paths that lead us away from those places as well*
> (STANLEY 2008, 14–15).

The word "intention" popped out. How often have I said I *intend* to do this or that and then failed to follow through? I *intended* to stay married for life. However, I lacked an understanding of the required commitment. I had no plan for the direction our lives would take to ensure we succeeded as a couple. I remember thinking that if only this book had been available to read earlier in our marriage, it might have prevented years of struggles.

Andy Stanley was right when he said that direction, an intentional choice, matters. Unfortunately, our "direction" was not focused on each other. Despite *intending* to be mutually respectful and supportive, we were drifting through life. As newlyweds, it was just the two of us. We hadn't discussed—much less planned—for life with the added responsibilities of increasing work demands, raising children, and all the family activities.

## BREAKING POINT

Jennifer's abduction was the emotional, physical, and spiritual last straw. At that moment, I had no idea what to do next. What change in *direction* would I have to make to avoid the destructive path I was on? I desperately wanted Jennifer to be brought home safely and to have the life she deserved. Feeling hopeless, I asked God to take my life so Jenn could have hers back. I remember thinking how much I would miss my wife and children, Matthew, Nicholas, and Morgan. I had reached rock bottom. Nowhere to go, helpless to control or change anything.

My prayer continued for a couple of weeks. Then, one day, I realized this was a ridiculous request. God wasn't going to answer it. Besides, why would He? After all, I walked away from Him nearly thirty-six years earlier.

So instead, I decided to face the brutal facts of my present reality: no more rationalizations or excuses. Looking in the mirror, I admitted to myself that I was selfish and self-centered.

One night, I remember experiencing peace during my conversation with God. It felt odd, bizarre. How could this be? How do I have peace when everything in my life is unraveling? What did this all mean? That would become a bit clearer in a couple of weeks.

## SELF-FOCUS IS UNHEALTHY

We all displayed this sense of *self* as young children, often aggressively. I lost count of the many times I heard my children say "mine," indicating possession of almost everything in their environment. Children also say "no" to anyone or anything that would take away what was theirs.

According to the *American Psychological Association Dictionary of Psychology*, self is "the totality of the individual, consisting of all characteristic attributes, conscious and unconscious, mental and physical. Carl Jung maintained that the self gradually develops by a process of individuation, which is not complete until late maturity is reached" (*APA Dictionary of Psychology*).

As adults, we mature and develop the ability to exercise control over our thoughts, desires, and actions. But, if we are honest with ourselves, it's an intentional choice when we don't exercise self-control. And generally, we will experience short-term or lasting consequences. The question we need to answer is, will we accept responsibility for not exercising self-control?

We ask ourselves, *Why am I here? What should I do for a living?* The focus is on "I" or "me."

Dr. Phil McGraw famously asked, "How is that working for you?" My answer? Two words: not good!

## DRIFTING OUT OF CONTROL

Early in our marriage, Debbie and I had an unintended barrier to spending quality time together. As a registered nurse, she worked shifts, including alternating weekends. In addition, I was in the United States Naval Reserve, which required drills every month and two weeks in the summer. Unfortunately, my weekend drills always seemed to fall when Debbie was off. And if that wasn't enough for two newlyweds, I worked for my father's business, which required extensive travel out of state.

In 1979, my sister Joyce and brother-in-law Drew moved to Barnegat, New Jersey. They selected a home on a cul-de-sac in a new community. Debbie and I visited often and liked the area. Within a few months after our wedding, we realized if we wanted to own a home, which we did, we couldn't afford to stay in our hometown areas. We decided to buy a house on the same street as Joyce and Drew in Barnegat. Our home was affordable, but we increased our commuting time. The first week of May 1981, we moved into our new home. My niece, Jennifer, was born two weeks later, on May 20, 1981. Our oldest, Matthew, was born in December 1983. Nick joined us in March 1987 and Morgan in September 1989.

As our children got older, I would step up to coach my kid's soccer teams, assist with little league baseball, and volunteer as a Boy Scouts leader.

I had transitioned to a new work role for the largest bank in New Jersey at the time. My territory included approximately thirty branches in two counties, requiring frequent travel to meet customers in one of our branch offices, homes, or businesses. My commitments and responsibilities were increasing. I struggled to manage time and expectations. My life felt like it was out of balance, like a snowball rolling down a hill aimlessly.

Eventually, I accepted the invitation to become the Boy Scouts district chairman, which required meeting with local troop leaders across the county and chairing an annual golf fundraising event. Successfully managing these roles led to an invitation to join the Jersey Shore council executive board as the vice president of the exploring program. Unfortunately, my life was veering off the tracks. That snowball just got bigger.

Without even realizing it, busyness fueled my ego. Being busy felt good; I was important. It filled a need to be wanted and valued.

Barnegat, like many fast-developing towns, was experiencing growing pains. The local government seemed unwilling or unable to take on important issues, such as building recreational spaces and schools to meet the increasing student population. We had a beachfront on Barnegat Bay with great views of the Barnegat Lighthouse on Long Beach Island. But, filled with debris and seaweed, it was an eyesore. It was not a place you wanted to bring your family.

I started attending the local government meetings, which became a source of frustration, as these elected officials were dismissive of the requests citizens made to improve the town. I would converse with neighbors before and after meetings. That led to an invitation to a local political club.

Before long, I was encouraged to run for office, which I did. Campaigns require a lot of time—meetings, phone calls, speaking engagements, and knocking on doors. From 1988 until 1993, I was involved in and helped run five primaries and five general election campaigns.

In 1989, I was elected to the Barnegat Township Committee (Council) and reelected in 1992. During those years, I took my responsibilities very seriously. I wanted to see meaningful progress in several areas to improve our community. As a result, more nights were spent out of the house, attending various meetings and fundraising events. My list of commitments was growing.

I worked closely with our county commissioners on several local projects, which led to an offer to become the next county director of the department of insurance and risk management. The county commissioner I reported to also served as the chairman of the local hospital board of trustees. Guess what happened next? Yup, he asked me to join the hospital board. Did *I* think about it? No. Did *I* discuss it with Debbie? No. *I* just said yes. I was always the people pleaser, but at what cost?

When family and friends looked at the calendar on our kitchen wall, they commented that every day of the week had multiple commitments. Just writing this, I'm exhausted thinking about how out of control my life had become.

All these to-dos were squeezing the happiness and joy out of my life.

*"There are two ways to be fooled. One is to believe what isn't true; the other is to refuse to believe what is true."*
—SOREN KIERKEGAARD (KIERKEGAARD 1962, 23)

My life reflected the choices *I* had made. Before making those decisions, *I* either didn't ask Debbie before *I* said yes, or *I* "sold" her on the decision. *I* rationalized these were opportunities for our family. *I* may have even convinced myself that it was true. But years later, upon reflection, it was a lie. Most of those choices, if not all of them, were for *me*.

### REFLECTIONS

Preparing for this chapter, and writing these words, was frankly embarrassing. Looking back and admitting that not only did I focus on *myself*, but worse, I rationalized it was really for my family. It's heartbreaking to think about the relational damage I caused my wife and children. Frankly, the newer version of me doesn't like the old version.

Reflecting on my *intentions* in all my relationships was also difficult to process. Andy Andrews wrote something that sums up this relational tension well:

*Have you ever considered how often we judge ourselves by our intentions while we judge others by their actions? Yet intention without action is an insult to those who expect the best from you* (ANDREWS 2009, 111).

That out-of-control snowball was increasing its speed and rolling over everything in its path. The question I never asked at the time was, what would happen when this messed-up life snowball hit an immovable object? Blindness to your reality does that. A real snowball will splatter, creating one heck of a scattered mess.

It may have appeared I was succeeding, but the reality was completely different. Internally, I felt a sense of frustration and helplessness about how to stop the madness.

Jennifer's abduction was a catalyst that forced me to face the truth about my life, my marriage, my family, and my work. As a result, I was emotionally, physically, and spiritually exhausted. As a man and husband, the weight of responsibility to have all the answers and lead my family was overwhelming. I felt ill-prepared and ill-equipped.

The fear of failing as a husband, father, and businessman consumed me. Outwardly, I displayed courage, confidence, and control. *I got this.* My life was a proverbial Hollywood set. It looked good from the outside, but behind the facade, it was an absolute mess.

How am I going to fix this? Where would I start? The principle of the path made sense. It offered guidance and hope. Would I have the courage to move in the right direction? I'm going to need help. Where or to whom could I turn?

# PART TWO

# INVITATIONS

# CHAPTER 3

# TO CHURCH

*I realize that so many people's main problem with
Christianity has far more to do with the church than with
Jesus. Ultimately faith and certainty grow as we get to
know more about Jesus, who he is, and what he did.*

—TIMOTHY KELLER

Our days seemed to mimic the plot in the movie *Groundhog
Day*. They just repeated themselves. I put my business activities on hold, thanks to my partners who picked up the slack.

During those first few weeks after Jennifer's abduction,
every restless night would give way to a new day. A fresh
start and the hope we would get some new answers about
Jenn's case. Every day my family and I, friends, and countless
volunteers would gather at the Mall at Millenia's community
center to organize activities for the day.

By this time, family and close friends were doing the
organizing. I began to act as the spokesman for our family so
Joyce, Drew, and Jenn's brother Logan could focus on media
and law enforcement meetings. I welcomed groups of volunteers and thanked them for their willingness to help us
find Jennifer. They would be directed to volunteers handing

out assignments for door knocking and missing person flyer distribution as we continued to spread out from Orlando into neighboring communities.

Unfortunately, we were not getting any closer to finding answers each day. Jennifer and the person of interest in the apartment complex surveillance video were still missing. But we gathered energy from one another and our common goal of finding Jenn. Seeing so many people who came to volunteer after hearing about Jenn's story on the news was invigorating. People we didn't know cared enough to help.

Soon after Jenn's abduction, Drew's boss invited Joyce and Drew to join his family at church that Sunday. They agreed and began regularly attending First Baptist Orlando. One evening after a long day, Joyce asked Debbie and me to join them. She shared how much she enjoyed attending services and how different it was from our childhood church in Hazlet, New Jersey.

The timing was perfect. Joyce didn't know anything about my nightly conversations with God, asking for His help. Little did I know He was pursuing me. He was answering me in ways I only would see later. This invitation was one of those ways.

As Debbie and I drove into the church campus, we were amazed by the sheer size of it. We saw several buildings and drove past a school building and sports fields. The parking lot was full of cars. Feeling a bit apprehensive, we walked toward the main church building. As we neared one of the entrances, the doors were opened by folks with smiling faces and warm greetings, welcoming us to the service that morning.

Debbie and I connected with Joyce and Drew in the upper balcony area. As I looked down and around, the church buzzed with activity. I could see people warmly greeting each other and having conversations—smiling faces were everywhere. By my estimate, a couple of thousand people were in the church that morning. On a large, raised platform, various musicians and singers were warming up and getting ready for the service to start.

Joyce was right. The church we grew up in was old, dark, and ominous. However, the atmosphere in this church was welcoming, bright, and inviting.

The service began with one of the pastors asking if any first-time guests had come. With hands raised around the room, the congregation burst out into applause. Next, the pastor asked everyone to greet the people near them and welcome them to the service. The loud buzz of voices echoed as people greeted each other.

*This is amazing. God must be in this place. This is how a church should be.*

The singing was powerful as I listened and read the words to the songs on big screens. As the music winded down, the pastor, Dr. David Uth, walked onto the platform, warmly welcomed everyone, and thanked the band and singers for leading worship.

Dr. Uth asked the congregation to open their Bibles to a specific passage. He then said something I'd never heard in church: "If you don't own a Bible, please take the one in the rack in front of you as our gift."

I picked up a Bible and went to the passage on the screen. I didn't take it home since we had one that was a wedding gift from Debbie's parents. Truthfully, I don't recall ever opening it except when we added our children's names on the family page after they were born.

As the pastor began his sermon, I listened intently. All these years later, I don't know what his message was about that Sunday, but I do remember how I felt and how emotional

I was. My heart raced, I had tears in my eyes, and I had no idea why. At one point, Debbie looked over at me and asked if everything was okay. I just nodded my head yes.

*Motivations are nearly always mixed. If you wait until your motives are pure and unselfish before you do something, you will wait forever. Nevertheless, it is important to ask what is primarily moving you toward an action, especially when it comes to faith commitment.*
—TIMOTHY KELLER (KELLER 2008, 227)

Something was happening. I just didn't know what it was at that moment. Something needed to change: me.

But how?

# CHAPTER 4

# AN UNEXPECTED INVITATION

*Progress is impossible without change, and those who
cannot change their minds cannot change anything.*

—GEORGE BERNARD SHAW

Something had stirred inside me. Every week, Debbie and I
continued to attend church services at First Orlando. And
every week, I was emotional. I looked forward to hearing
the pastor's messages weekly and reading the Bible passages.
I sang with everyone else for the first time and enjoyed it.
After the service, Debbie and I would share our thoughts on
the message. We both felt like we were learning about God,
His plans, and His purposes as the pastor would connect each
sermon to practical aspects of life.

On Palm Sunday, April 9, 2006, Debbie had to work, so
I went to church alone. My sister Joyce and Drew had gone
back home to Bradenton for the weekend. After the service, I
drove home on I-4 and experienced something that had never
happened before. My eyes were on the road, but in my mind,
I saw random images of memories rapidly flashing in front of
me. Then, suddenly, those images disappeared, replaced by
"hearing" a clear message.

*Call Bill Rush.*
*Call Bill Rush.*
*Call Bill Rush.*

Without exaggeration, that message repeated throughout the rest of the day. And it was the first thing I "heard" after waking up early on Monday, April 10. So, I called Bill. He immediately answered the phone. After a brief conversation, we planned to have lunch at Carmela's Restaurant in his company's office complex.

I struggled to comprehend what was happening after I hung up with Bill that Monday morning. While sitting and having coffee, I reflected on the time Bill and I worked together at a workers' compensation services company in Longwood, Florida.

I remembered Bill as a humble, gentle, kind, and caring man. He had the heart of a servant and stood out because of his quiet demeanor. I looked forward to seeing him again.

I arrived early at Carmela's. After we sat, Bill asked how Debbie, I, and the kids were doing, then about Joyce and Drew. Jennifer's case was regularly in the local news. By April, billboards and large vinyl missing person signs with Jennifer's picture were all over the greater Orlando area.

"I'm praying for Jennifer and your family," Bill told me gently, looking into my eyes with concern. Our conversation quickly turned as Bill sensed my grief, helplessness, and despair. Then, in a moment of rare vulnerability, I shared with Bill those nightly conversations with God. Without even thinking, I told him about asking God to take my life so Jennifer could have hers back.

Bill listened intently and compassionately and then asked if I regularly attended church. I shared how Joyce and Drew connected with First Baptist Orlando on the last Sunday of

January and how Debbie and I had been attending for about two months.

One issue kept bouncing around in my mind. Do I tell Bill about what happened on the way home from church the day before? Honestly, "seeing" those memories and "hearing" what seemed like an audible voice telling me to call him was a bit too much to process, let alone share with anyone. But then, I suddenly felt a pronounced nudge, a prompt:

*Just tell Bill.*

With a bit of hesitancy, I chose my words deliberately and described to Bill what had happened on the drive home after the Palm Sunday services.

"You're not surprised?" I stared at him in disbelief.

"No," he said. "Based upon what you just shared, it sounds like God is seeking to get your attention. He's stirred up your past memories for a reason and prompted you to call me." He grinned. "I'm honored and glad you called."

We spent three hours together that afternoon. Bill shared the love and hope offered by Jesus to everyone who would answer His call in their lives. He shared how God has plans and purposes for me, and while it wasn't clear at this moment, His plans are perfect, as is His timing.

I asked him, "What am I to do now?"

He still wore the same grin. "Accept Jesus' invitation. Open your heart to Him. Allow Him to begin working in you."

I nodded yes.

"Great. Would you be okay with me offering a prayer?" His eyes narrowed on me.

"Yes. Of course."

Bill reached across the table with open hands. We grasped each other's hands, and he offered a prayer. I asked Jesus to come into my life. And to help me become a better husband and father.

Bill's eyes and smile spoke loudly. He reached over, shook my hand, and congratulated me. Then, he asked, "Do you have a Bible at home?"

"We have the one given to us by Debbie's parents on our wedding day, but it's too hard to read," I replied.

Bill suggested, "Go to a bookstore, skim through a few Bibles, and buy the one you find easiest to read. Today was the easy part. Now you have work to do. It is essential that you commit to reading your Bible every day. It's the only way you will understand who God is and the plans He has for you." Bill offered to help in any way he could and suggested we set a plan to meet regularly.

I was amazed at Bill's passion and confidence as he talked about God and the Bible. "Where in the Bible should I start?"

He said, "I would suggest reading the Gospel of Matthew first and then the other gospels because they will introduce you to Jesus and why He came to Earth."

As we were finishing our time together, Bill shared he was a leader with Bible Study Fellowship. His church in Winter Park hosted the evening men's class. He shared how much he had learned and matured in his faith through the weekly group meetings. He invited me to join the group when the new study year started in September.

Our time together went by fast; the conversation was like drinking from a fire hose, but it exhilarated me. I experienced peace and calmness that had been elusive for many months. At 3 p.m., we ended our time together. A simple "thank you" was undoubtedly inadequate as we embraced each other. I looked forward to our next meeting.

Now that I had invited God into my life, I felt a sense of walking into the unknown, a level of excitement and hesitancy. The prospect of change can do that. I was thankful to have a mentor walking with me, and as Bill said, Jesus would also be with me. I had no idea what that meant and what it would look like, but I was excited to take my next steps.

## REFLECTIONS

That April afternoon, I was just over six weeks shy of turning fifty years old. It was hard to believe I had lived a half-century and now found myself wrestling with my reality. And preparing to embark on a quest to learn more about God.

*What did I want out of life? Who did I want to be?* A man of integrity. A good father. A loving husband. A caring friend. *Why did it take Jennifer's abduction to open my eyes and heart to realize what I truly valued: my family?* In December, divorce had been a real possibility. Now I had to fight to save my marriage.

Answering God's call gave me hope. I committed myself to begin listening and learning. I had no idea how this was going to play out. Or where God would take me. I felt a bit uncomfortable and unsettled. However, contrasted with my messed-up life, it was the only wise choice. Truthfully, the fear of the *known* was more frightening.

My good friend John Mattone is a brilliant executive coach. He served the late Steve Jobs, the legendary former CEO of PepsiCo Roger Enrico, and countless global and government leaders. Yet John remains grounded in who he is as a person. He has a passion for excellence and is an enthusiastic encourager. In his book *The Intelligent Leader,* he said something I remind myself of often:

*Seeing clearly is important, but unless you're willing to take action on what you see, then you won't progress. This is where the rubber meets the road. If you are able to see and acknowledge that something needs to change, then you need to take the courageous leap into action.*

—JOHN MATTONE (MATTONE 2020, 129)

Life was already changing rapidly, and I didn't want to miss a better future. For twenty-plus years, my church attendance was the obligatory Christmas and Easter Mass. I now looked forward to attending church and learning through the practical teaching of Dr. Uth. His weekly words penetrated my heart and mind.

We live in the fine lines of relational tension. Like good card players, we show what we want, keeping the truth close to our chests. We don't open the door to our inner self wide enough for people to get a look at the mess within. Yet, I was about to take the doors off my life to get honest with what was inside me.

Keeping my thoughts to myself made me feel like I was in control—even though I knew it was a lie. *How am I going to come clean? How will my conversations with Debbie go?* I was scared to be that vulnerable. If Bill could have peace, joy, and contentment, then it was possible for me. He trusts God, so I decided to trust God.

Trusting God would mean spending time learning about Him. That required new priorities and boundaries. Getting up early in the morning offered me quiet time to read my Bible and to reflect on the passages. I knew if I didn't set aside the first part of the day, work, the kids' activities, and general busyness would take over. Getting up before the rest of the family created a space for focused time that did not interfere with family or work responsibilities.

The following weeks and months were challenging. I discovered the brutal facts of my life. Occasionally, I pushed back. But despite my denials or attempts to feel better about myself, I *was* self-centered.

Bill's act of kindness created a pivotal moment in my life. With weekly encouragement and a commitment to change, I was on a mission and chose courage over comfort.

CHAPTER 5

# TO BIBLE STUDY

*Every experience in your life, is preparing you for what's to come.*
*When you look back over seasons that you may have thought*
*were wasted, you were building character for where you are now.*
—BRYAN L. CARTER

On Monday, September 11, 2006, the United States remembered
the attack on our country five years earlier. A sad reminder
that our world is broken and dangerous, divided by man-cre-
ated ethnic, cultural, and religious barriers to meaningful and
lasting peace. A world where people struggle to find identity,
self-worth, acceptance, and relational connection. Tension
and hostility leave many people feeling helpless and hopeless.

This Monday, with memories of 9/11 and Jenn's abduction
freshly imprinted on my mind, I began a new journey to finding
hope. Bill Rush invited me to join him at Bible Study Fellowship
International's (BSF) men's bible study hosted at the Winter
Park Baptist Church. We arranged to meet before class. As
we walked in together, I saw men and children everywhere
I looked. I felt a palpable buzz of excitement, smiling faces,
and laughter. Men and kids were reconnecting after the long
summer break.

Bill brought me to the sanctuary, where a small group of "new" men assembled for a short briefing on the BSF study model. We learned our personal study was reinforced weekly through four touch points: answering questions, small group discussion, listening to a lecture, and reading commentary notes. In addition, this class had over three-hundred men and one-hundred children participating in this study of Romans written by the apostle Paul. Marc Stanakis led my group of ten guys. Over the next thirty-two weeks, we would study, share, and pray for each other.

That first night, each man in the group shared a little about themselves—their walk with God and why they had signed up for this study. I briefly shared my story, including Jennifer's abduction and meeting with Bill Rush. The entire group had heard about Jenn from the news. Many knew Bill from his involvement in BSF.

By the second week, I felt overwhelmed and inadequate in trying to keep up with the daily questions. This was a serious Bible study. How serious? Consider the first chapter's message to the followers of Jesus in Rome:

I am not ashamed of this Good News about Christ. It is the power of God at work, saving everyone who believes... This Good News tells us how God makes us right in his sight. This is accomplished from start to finish by faith. But God shows his anger from heaven against all sinful, wicked people who suppress the truth by their wickedness. They know the truth about God because he has made it obvious to them. For ever since the world was created, people have seen the earth and sky. Through everything God made, they can clearly see his invisible qualities—his eternal power and divine nature. So they have no excuse for not knowing God. (Romans 1:16-20, NLT)

Good news. God's anger. No excuse for not knowing God. It was as if Paul was speaking directly to me.

I sat and listened to the other men answer the questions over the next two weeks. Again, I felt the anxiety and inadequacy swelling up inside.

*I can't do this. I'm in over my head. What was I thinking?* I felt like I was drowning, becoming hopeless. I wanted to be encouraged. Instead, I felt inept. *I gave this my best shot. Tonight will be my last night. What will I tell Bill? I'll figure that out later.* My demeanor and facial grimaces gave me away.

After our group discussion, Marc approached me. "Hey, Bill. I'd love to grab coffee with you one morning. How does this Thursday look for you?"

*Did Marc read my mind?* With momentary relief, I said, "Yes, thanks. That would be great. Where do you want to meet, and what time is good for you?"

Marc shot back, "How about Starbucks on 17/92 in Winter Park? Let's plan on 8 a.m."

"Perfect," I replied. "I'll look forward to seeing you on Thursday."

Thursday arrived. Rather than feeling anxious, I was excited to get to know Marc. We got our coffee, sat down, and exchanged small talk. Marc then asked, "So, how's it going? You have been looking a bit overwhelmed."

I smiled and said, "That would be an understatement. I'm struggling to understand what we're reading. And answering the questions."

"You're not alone," Marc said. "Many of the guys attending BSF started with limited or no Bible knowledge, including myself." Then Marc, smiling, said, "Most of them only came because their wives attend the women's class and began bugging them to go to the men's class."

Marc's words were comforting and reassuring.

"Don't give up," Marc continued. "You are on a personal journey. God has you here for a reason. He won't let you down."

"I know this seems difficult, but it's also worth it. Keep investing your time. Day by day, over the weeks, you'll notice that what you're reading will start making more sense." Marc confidently stated, "Go easy on yourself. Be patient."

By the end of the first semester in mid-December, I felt better about the process. More confident. The lessons were engaging, and I looked forward to each week's discussion time. Something inside me confirmed that studying *Romans* was the right starting point for my new faith journey.

The year 2006 was almost over, and January 24, 2007, was quickly approaching. Our family was about to relive the events and emotions of Jennifer's abduction. A year later, and no closer to understanding what happened and where she might be. I reflected on the past year, but through a new lens: the Bible. Paul's words were still relevant two thousand years later.

I felt a prompt to write a letter from my heart to our Central Florida community, which I did. It was published in the *Orlando Sentinel* on December 22, 2006, with the title, "Making Sense of Jennifer Kesse Tragedy,"

*I am the uncle of Jennifer Kesse, who has been missing from Orlando since Jan. 24.*

*On Christmas Eve, it will be 11 months since Jennifer's life and the lives of everyone who knows and loves her changed. So many questions, so few answers. Someone out there knows something. We pray that God touches their hearts so that they come forward with the information that will bring Jennifer home safely. This is our only Christmas wish.*

*That Tuesday began like many days as Jennifer was preparing for work. A college graduate with a good job and a new home, she was living the American dream. Loved by her family, friends, and boyfriend, her future was so promising.*

*It was all gone in a moment.*

*How do we make sense of such tragedies? We ask ourselves, "Why did God allow this to happen?" Jennifer's tragedy made me determined to answer questions instead of asking them.*

*A special connection was made with First Baptist Church of Orlando, whose membership warmly embraces our family and supports us through prayer and outreach. Attending services renews our spirits, touches our hearts and gives us hope. Sermon messages were hitting home. Something was happening inside of me.*

*For the first time, I made a serious attempt to read my Bible, and quickly began to see parallels of circumstances in my life playing out before me. The more I read, the more I wanted to know. Then it hit me: This book contained solutions to daily challenges. It is life's instruction manual, a gift from God to all of us. For the first time, I realized that He wants us to know Him, to have a relationship with Him. Most important, I realized how little control over my life I actually have and that I needed help.*

*Regrets?*

*Only one: that it took 50 years to realize this.*

*Our family has so much to be thankful for this year. Our hearts were touched by the overwhelming support from the community of Orlando—law enforcement, residents, media and businesses who assisted a family they did not know. In fact, people from across our state, as well as visitors from other states and abroad, volunteered time to assist efforts to find Jennifer.*

*My Christmas wish to everyone is this: Focus your life on what really matters—relationships, not stuff. Recognize we all need help—life is a team sport.*

*Today, not tomorrow, hug someone you know and tell that person how much you love him or her. Mend a relationship with a neighbor, co-worker or family member—you may not get the chance tomorrow.*

*As you prepare to put together all of the gifts with "some assembly required," remember that an instruction manual is provided for a reason. And the greatest instruction manual of all, is the Bible. God knew our lives would not be easy, and that we would face daily challenges; that's why he provided the manual for us. Please don't wait until all else fails to read these instructions.*

*From our family to yours, please accept our heartfelt prayers for peace, hope and joy—each and every day.*
(GILMOUR 2006)

I couldn't have written that letter if it were not for the transformation that began to take shape after Jenn's abduction. And without the support of many people who walked with me on this new quest. I am incredibly grateful Marc stepped in when he did and encouraged me to continue studying with my men's group. As a result, I better understood my life and God's story.

With God's inspiration, I had the confidence to write this letter. At the time, I didn't know if the *Orlando Sentinel* would publish it. I needed to write it for myself. To express the hope I was beginning to feel.

I wanted desperately to make a difference in the lives of my family. As Bryan Carter said, "Everything I experienced and learned was preparation for the future."

## INVITED TO SERVE

In April of 2007, Marc Stanakis asked me to stay for a few minutes after our group time. When we were alone, he asked me something I had never expected in a million years: "Bill, would you be willing to consider meeting with Ed Wood [the class teaching leader] to discuss joining our leadership team?"

I felt the blood rush out of me. My grayish face betrayed me. "Excuse me. What?" I responded. "Me? I've only been studying the Bible since September."

Smiling, Marc said, "I've observed significant growth in you since you started. Week by week, your passion, enthusiasm, and desire to learn are evident. Please pray about it this week. We'll talk next Monday."

I was flattered but still felt inadequate. Mark's kind words were encouraging. That night, as I prayed, my doubts began to dissipate. I told Marc the next class night, "I would be honored to meet with Ed."

My mind raced as I drove to the meeting. *What is he going to ask me to do? I am okay working with men. But please don't ask me to work with kids.*

I felt comfortable sharing my doubts and concerns with Ed. "This has been overwhelming. I'm still trying to process what happened over the past year," I said with a hint of nervousness, "And my prayer list has grown to the point it feels like a burden. How do I manage it all?"

"Everything you're experiencing is perfectly normal," he assured me. "It's a process that takes time. And you have God as your teacher."

Ed smiled. "I know exactly how you feel. Let me share my thoughts. First, if someone asks you to pray for them, tell them they must keep you updated on what's happening. That sets mutual expectations." Next, he shared, "Create a journal to write the prayers, names, and dates. Leave space to write the answers and include dates. Doing this will make praying less stressful." Ed concluded, "Over time, you will be able to go back and be encouraged by God's faithfulness through answered prayer."

With relief, I said, "Thanks, Ed. That was very helpful."

"Do you have any other questions or concerns?'" Ed asked.

"No, I'm good," I replied.

"Great," Ed responded. "Thank you for meeting with me and praying about joining our class leadership group. How would you feel about working in our school program?"

*Working with kids! No, that wasn't my first choice.* With some hesitancy, I said, "Well, I thought I'd be working with men. But if the need is with kids, I'm okay with that. Yeah, if that is the need, that'll be fine."

"Terrific. I'll look forward to you joining us this Saturday morning. We meet from 5:30 a.m. to 8 a.m. Arrive a little earlier so I can brief you on the meeting schedule," Ed said as he welcomed me to my new role in the class.

I met with thirty-five men on Saturday mornings for the remainder of the class year as we prepared for Monday class nights. Saturday mornings became the highlight of my week. On Monday evenings, I sat in and observed the different school program grade levels.

## LEARNING FROM CHILDREN

*We should ask God to increase our hope when it*
*is small, awaken it when it is dormant, confirm*
*it when it is wavering, strengthen it when it is*
*weak, and raise it up when it is overthrown.*

—JOHN CALVIN (CALVIN AND KUNTZE 2020)

Excitement and expectancy were in the air. I was excited to be back studying the Bible with my men's group in the Orlando Evening Men's class and expecting God to show up and show me something new about Himself.

In September 2007, we began studying the Gospel of Matthew. I would be serving as a leader in our children's program. I didn't expect God to reveal what a genuine heart for Him looked like in a group of young middle school-aged boys and girls.

In his article "The Value of Children in Antiquity," Titus Kennedy wrote, "In ancient Israel, children were usually seen as a blessing from God. The Mosaic Law also protected children, even those who were orphans. This was in stark contrast to the prevailing views circulating in the Roman Empire and beyond during the 1st century."

How stark? Pagan cultures often dedicated their children to serve the gods in various ways, the worst being sacred prostitution and human sacrifice. And these would be seen as "honorable" for children. However, children generally did not have high intrinsic value. Society accepted a concept called "exposure," where unwanted children would be left outside to die (Kennedy 2018).

Matthew, a Jewish boy, was born in that culture. As an adult, his fellow Jews despised him for working with the Roman Empire as a tax collector. Then, one day, he had a life-changing encounter with Jesus, who asked him to "follow Me." Matthew did, and over nearly three years, he listened to Jesus' teachings, watched His actions, and wrote down what he heard and observed. One day Jesus' followers asked him,

> "Who is the greatest in the kingdom of heaven?" And calling to him a child, he put him in the midst of them and said, "Truly, I say to you, unless you turn and become like children, you will never enter the kingdom of heaven. Whoever humbles himself like this child is the greatest in the kingdom of heaven." (MATTHEW 18:1-4, ESV)

Prevailing cultural preferences placed little to no value on children. Yet Jesus' astonishing words revealed the heart of His Father.

### EYEWITNESS TESTIMONY AND EVIDENCE

While studying Matthew's eyewitness account of Jesus' life, I was struck by the details and evidence presented. He knew the supernatural acts he was observing needed to be documented accurately. This Jesus he was following was the kindest, most loving, and gentle man he had ever known. His compassion was limitless to friend and foe. Jesus revealed His power over nature, disease, and death. Matthew came to know Jesus *was* the promised Messiah.

He and the other Gospel writers were intentional in providing evidence that proved what they knew and had observed. Importantly, many eyewitnesses to these events were alive and could verify the accuracy. Jesus:

*Turned water to wine at a wedding in Cana*
*Healed a royal official's son who was*
*near death in Capernaum*
*Drove a demon spirit from a man in Capernaum*
*Provided a miraculous catch of fish for Peter*
*and his associates on Lake Gennesaret*
*Healed a man covered with leprosy*
*Healed a centurion's servant near death in Capernaum*
*Healed a paralyzed man who had been carried*
*by his friends, witnessed by religious leaders*
*Raised a woman's son who had died to new life in Nain*
*Calmed a lake storm that threatened His followers*
*Raised the daughter of Jairus, a synagogue*
*ruler, to life after she had died*
*Healed two blind men*
*Fed thousands of people at different times*
*Healed ten lepers while traveling to Jerusalem*
*Raised his friend Lazarus from death to life*
*Healed Malchus' ear, which had been cut off by Peter*
*during His arrest in the Garden of Gethsemane*

John wrote, "Jesus did many other things as well. If every one of them were written down, I suppose that even the whole world would not have room for the books that would be written" (John 20:25, NIV).

### REFLECTION

It was becoming clear Jesus was God in human flesh.

How much more evidence do you need to make your decision about Jesus? We have two options: Jesus is who He claimed to be, or He is a liar. He did not give us other options to consider.

In the Introduction, we read the apostle John's *big idea*: that *you* and *I* may *believe* "that Jesus is the Christ, the Son of God" (John 20:31, NCV).

Seeing the passages come alive in those young boys and girls made a lasting impression as I matured in my relationship with God. Over the weeks, I watched and listened as these middle schoolers taught me through their humility, open hearts, and eager desire to learn.

I still felt a bit overwhelmed during the first semester. A new student of the Bible myself, I was now part of team-teaching middle school students. Bob Berry was my coleader. His warm smile, kindness, and gentleness were calming, and he had a grandfatherly way about him. He had been in the program for quite a few years. So many of his former students would come up and hug him. Bob encouraged me every week during training and on class nights.

Without a doubt, I learned more from those kids than they likely learned from me. Listening to them respond to the lessons was a vivid illustration and reminder of how I needed to approach my studies: with awe and wonder in my eyes, heart, and mind.

Week by week, my confidence grew. I found a rhythm in my study time that worked. I would get up early, around 4:30 a.m., make a cup of coffee, and begin reading my Bible and answering questions. Afterward, I felt energized and ready to take on the day.

However, questions remained as my reasoning wrestled with the concept of accepting the passages we were studying by faith.

*The paradox between divine sovereignty and human responsibility. This is an apparent paradox—not a true paradox, but an apparent paradox—which*

*faith accepts while reason rejects. Faith accepts,*
*because faith acknowledges that we don't have all*
*the information, but we trust God. Faith accepts this.*
*Reason rejects it, and that's because reason is finite.*

—JOHN MACARTHUR (MACARTHUR 2008)

I was encouraged and enthusiastic about how things were going in my life. However, deep in the recesses of my heart, unbearable pain and a sense of loss remained. If God is sovereign, then why did this happen to Jennifer? Not knowing continued to haunt me.

# PART THREE

# LISTENING

## CHAPTER 6

# LISTENING IS CHALLENGING

*People love to talk but hate to listen. Listening is not merely
not talking, though even that is beyond most of our powers;
it means taking a vigorous, human interest in what is being
told us. You can listen like a blank wall or like a splendid
auditorium where every sound comes back fuller and richer.*

—ALICE DUER MILLER

Something was happening inside me that I didn't understand
and couldn't explain. Debbie and I continued attending services
at First Baptist Orlando. Every week, I became emotional as I
listened to the music, hymns, and discussions of Bible passages.

Church services felt more like a class in school you looked
forward to every week. I sat on the edge of my seat, leaning in
to hear every word. One week I brought a small notebook to
write down my thoughts and key takeaways from the sermon
messages. I listened purposefully instead of half-heartedly.

Every week, the messages caused a palpable feeling of
having a finger poked into areas of my life I didn't want to
address and had ignored. Truths that had been hidden or
buried. Listening to Pastor Uth's words, those truths came
to the surface. I knew I needed to deal with them. I heard
the words and felt them in my heart and soul. So, I listened

carefully, genuinely seeking to understand what it all meant. Would these words help me in a way I could apply to my life to become a better person?

One of those truths was acknowledging when Debbie would share something challenging that happened with the kids or at work. My response was to jump into fix-it mode without listening carefully to the conversation. Instead, I quickly offered solutions. And that was a problem. Operating on autopilot, I would typically hear something, say something, and then move on.

Reflecting on past conversations, I treated them more like projects to be completed. Get in, get done, and get on to something else. There's that finger poke. Looking back, my engagement during discussions, especially with Debbie, often lacked empathy, genuine concern, compassion, and sensitivity. That's painful to admit, but it was true. I'm shaking my head at the countless times this pattern has played out in my life. Why did I do it? Why do any of us do it?

Honest conversations include at least two people in a discussion, with active participation and sharing. What had I been doing? Just *reacting* to words being spoken. I wasn't fully participating *in* the conversation.

> Sometimes all a person wants is an empathetic
> ear; all he or she needs is to talk it out. Just offering
> a listening ear and an understanding heart for
> his or her suffering can be a big comfort.
> —ROY T. BENNETT (BENNETT 2011)

It's hard to be empathetic, understanding, and comforting when you focus on yourself. Unfortunately, one of the unintended consequences of self-centeredness is we don't listen well. And it's frustrating when it happens to us. We recognize when someone is engaged in a conversation or if they appear to be daydreaming. In my case, I was likely thinking about the next thing *I* wanted to say.

To every person in my life reading this book, please accept my heartfelt apology for not being a better listener. I'm working on becoming more other-focused so that I'm empathetic, understanding, and comforting the next time we talk.

In an article by Neil Katz and Kevin McNulty at Syracuse University, "Reflective Listening," the authors wrote:

*Listening is following the thoughts and feelings of another and understanding what the other is saying from his or her perspective. Reflective listening is a special type of listening that involves paying respectful attention to the content and feeling expressed in another persons' communication. Reflective listening is hearing and understanding, and then letting the other know that he or she is being heard and understood. It requires responding actively to another while keeping your attention focused completely on the speaker.* (KATZ AND MCNULTY 1994)

Knowing this would have prevented hundreds, if not thousands, of stress-filled conversations and the relational tension that followed with Debbie and others. The authors point out that reflective listening is about focusing intentionally on the other person and what they say. It's not going to be easy. I'd need a lot of practice not responding immediately—learning to relax, lean in, and listen carefully would be a good start.

*Listen with curiosity. Speak with honesty. Act with integrity. The greatest problem with communication*

*is we don't listen to understand. We listen to reply.*
*When we listen with curiosity, we don't listen with the*
*intent to reply. We listen for what's behind the words.*
—ROY T. BENNETT (BENNETT 2019)

I want my marriage and other relationships to be the best they can be and mutually encouraging. For that to be true, I must be a fully engaged, active listener who is curious, responds honestly, and acts with integrity. I am thankful for every finger poke I get that points out an area of my life that needs rehabilitation.

It's sobering to look in the mirror and face reality. As I recalled countless conversations with Debbie, I was heartbroken about how my body language, tone, and callous words were insensitive and disrespectful. And worse were the times I acted genuinely interested while having a conversation but was preoccupied with other things. Ouch. If I had treated Debbie this way, could I have done the same to others?

Life transformation is a painful process that takes time, patience, humility, and understanding from everybody involved. I wondered how Debbie had put up with me all these years.

## ADDICTIVE DISTRACTIONS, UNSEEN CONSEQUENCES
We have another conversational challenge to be aware of: our cell phones.

Any technology can work for or against us. Unfortunately, we may not be aware of the against us part or realize what is happening. Our mobile devices make contacting people more accessible and convenient. Smartphones created a massive shift in how we work and interact with mobile phones and people.

However, our dependence on smartphones is habit-forming for many of us. And habits can lead to addiction.

You're probably reading this thinking I'm crazy. People don't get "addicted" to phones. Really? Look around you. Everywhere you go, people have a phone in their hands. You see it outside walking. In shopping malls and restaurants. In your home and bed. And in supermarkets. Why are we having loud conversations while pushing a cart in the grocery store?

Still not convinced? Just observe how people respond when they hear their notification sounds. It reminds me of how the doctor checks our knee reflexes. The knee gets hit with the little hammer, and up goes the leg. Hear a notification sound and reach for the phone. And it's not just notifications on our phones; it's on our computers. Start observing the people you're with; the second a notification sound goes off, they respond. They might be in a conversation with you, but they respond as soon as those sounds go off. It's incredible to watch, and it's frustrating and disrespectful.

Another "addiction" that impacts our communication and listening efforts is social media platforms. It never occurred to me that social media platforms like Facebook, Twitter, and Instagram are like drug pushers. These platforms encourage and entice people to use their services, and once you get *hooked*, they will make a lot of money off your usage.

If you think I'm making this up, consider this: have you ever searched for a particular product or hotel and airline for a trip? We all have. But have you noticed that ads immediately start popping up for exact products or services on your social media pages?

*Lost in Space* was my favorite TV show growing up in the 1960s. A robot warned of unseen dangers. I think we would all appreciate that kind of help. In a future chapter, we'll learn we have someone better than a robot.

Speaking about unseen dangers. Catherine Price wrote in her article "Trapped—the Secret Ways Social Media Is Built to Be Addictive (And What You Can Do to Fight Back)" that "social media isn't designed with your long-term happiness in mind" (Price 2018).

How often have you been using your phone or playing a video game and suddenly realized you just lost a big block of time? We all have, but with phones in hand, we just keep scrolling.

In her article, Catherine warns us of the dangers we can't see and their consequences. She wrote, "While we're busy burying our noses in our newsfeeds, a strange thing is going on in Silicon Valley: tech insiders have begun to speak out against some of the very products they helped create."

Consider the following statements by social media leaders:

*Chamath Palihapitiya, Facebook's former vice president for use growth, was speaking at Stanford University's School of Business when he said, "I feel tremendous guilt...I think we have created tools that are ripping apart the social fabric of how society works." He added that he rarely uses Facebook and that his children "aren't allowed to use that sh\*t."*

*Sean Parker, founding president of Facebook, said that social media "literally changes your relationship with society, with each other. It probably interferes with productivity in weird ways. God only knows what it's doing to our children's brains."*

*And Tim Cook, Apple's chief executive, said that when it comes to his nephew, "there are some things that I won't allow. I don't want them on a social network"* (PRICE 2018).

We should all be alarmed if this is what a company founder and senior executives say. I hear a robot warning us of danger ahead.

Why are they concerned?

Catherine pointed out Facebook is free to use "because we are not the customers...advertisers are the customers, and our attention is what's being sold." Our experiences on social media confirm this. The more time you and I spend engaged with social media, the more advertisements are offered to us. Catherine continued, "We need to remember why social media companies would want to get us hooked in the first place...every minute you spend on social media is a minute spent making money for someone else" (Price 2018).

Since my goal is to learn to listen better, I must recognize and remove anything in my life that distracts me from listening reflectively.

In a previous chapter, we discussed the principle of the path: "Direction, not intention, determines our destination" (Stanley 2018). I don't recall deciding to get hooked on my phone or social media, but it happened. If we aren't anchored correctly and have not set a destination, we will end up somewhere we wouldn't have chosen.

**REFLECTIONS**

During the global COVID-19 shutdown, I spent a lot of time outdoors walking and became a huge fan of audiobooks and podcasts.

On August 31, 2020, I listened to *Business Made Simple with Donald Miller.* This episode was titled "The Secret to Staying Focused at Work" (Miller 2020). Donald's guest was Nir Eyal, the author of *Indistractable.*

That day, my life changed. During the podcast, the conversation centered on the distractions we allow in our lives, and Nir offered solutions. At the podcast's end, I immediately downloaded his book on Audible and began listening to Nir's story. Takeaways included that we have too many distractions in our lives, and the ability to stay focused can be an advantage in life and work. One highlight for me was recognizing an increasing demand for my attention and the importance of leveraging technology for my good without allowing it to take over my life.

Nir's message and research were so compelling I immediately took advantage of the tools offered and began the process of reclaiming time by removing distractions. That decision more than two years ago has helped me in many areas of my life, including writing this book. Most importantly, it helped me engage more in conversations, free of external distractions. In addition, by turning off all notifications on my cell phone and computer, I no longer responded to the endless stimuli from these devices, ending the unplanned interruptions in my day.

I highly recommend you get the book. This is so important; put this book down and order *Indistractable.* It may help you get the most out of this book and prevent you from drifting off into danger.

One of my favorite authors, Bob Goff, recently wrote a book, *Undistracted: Capture Your Purpose, Rediscover Your Joy.* Bob wrote,

*Here's a truth you can take to the bank no matter how long you live: The clarity of purpose, undistracted energy, selfless love, and unselfish pursuits you bring to the world will be your legacy. Everything else will look like a distraction by comparison.* (GOFF 2022, 21)

Bob's words encouraged me to stay focused, be clear about my purpose, and love people well.

Every day, we face unseen dangers. And we suffer the consequences of ignoring our internal warning bells and the counsel of other people. The good news is we have access to someone who knows our past, present, and future and wants to help us avoid unwise choices.

We hear words all day, every day. The challenge is actively listening. To what or to whom are we listening? Learning to listen to the right words is critical to our emotional well-being. In the next chapter, we will learn about the importance and impact of words on people.

# CHAPTER 7

# WORDS MATTER

*Words start wars and end them, create love and choke it, bring us to laughter and joy and tears. Words cause men and women to willingly risk their lives, their fortunes and their sacred honor. Our world, as we know it, revolves on the power of words.*

—ROY WILLIAMS

Words are not inherently good or bad. However, in the wrong hands, with the wrong motives, they can be weaponized. Words can be like sticks of dynamite, blowing up relationships. Maybe it would be helpful if dictionaries came with a disclaimer:

WARNING: This package's content can be dangerous to your health. Handle with care. Don't use contents when tired, stressed, angry, or hungry. Use can be harmful to people within range of your voice. Research has shown the effects of inappropriate use of words may not be immediate. Studies have determined the damage can last for an entire lifetime.

While a parody, I believe the warning is appropriate. We know that, if mishandled, words can blow up relationships and lives. The warning label should also include the recommendation for personal protective equipment for hearing. Unfortunately, we can't put positive self-image, confidence, wisdom, and discernment into our ears. They must be in our hearts. We'll talk about that later.

## WORDS CAN IMPACT DECISIONS

Every day, we make decisions based on words. Ideally, we want to trust those words are true or accurate.

Seven years before Jennifer's abduction, I was offered a new job opportunity. But unfortunately, it would require our family to relocate to Longwood, Florida, near Orlando. Our families and friends have all lived in New Jersey our entire lives. After twenty-one years as a nurse, Debbie had her dream job with a well-known cardiology practice. In addition, our children were all in school and involved with other activities.

During the in-person interviewing process, everything went well. The people were great, enthusiastic, and professional. The company was a workers' compensation third-party administrator, a division of a large national healthcare insurance company. They were investing in and committed to the growth of this division. Sounded good so far. The words I heard were encouraging. This was going to be a big decision. At the time, I worked for a large county in New Jersey. Working in government is generally safe, stable, and secure.

So, based on the words I heard, the Gilmour family decided to take the opportunity, and we moved to our new home in Lake Mary, Florida, in April 1999. The following month, I was in a leadership meeting. The executive director told the management team that our parent company would sell our division. *Wait, what?* It's only been a month since my family moved to Florida. Anxiety washed over me. What was I going to tell Debbie and the kids? As a man of courage, I didn't say anything. Based on the timetable presented, I knew this would take a while, so I rationalized, *Why create stress for everyone by sharing his news now?*

The truth is I was afraid that if I shared this news with Debbie, she would shoot me—figuratively, of course. We moved over one thousand miles. She left her family, her dream job, and our previous life—for me. All because I was excited about the opportunity based on the representations and words I heard. Words *can* change the course of our lives.

## WORDS THAT ENCOURAGE

In the fall of 2010, Debbie and I received an invitation to a fundraising event in Tampa. One of the speakers was Danny Wuerffel, a former quarterback and Heisman Trophy winner at the University of Florida. He also played in the National Football League with several teams, including the New Orleans Saints. While in New Orleans, Danny volunteered with Desire Street Ministries, a local nonprofit working to bring spiritual renewal and community improvements to poverty-stricken neighborhoods after the devastation brought to the area by Hurricane Katrina. After retiring from the NFL, Danny became the executive director of Desire Street Ministries.

One of the most important things I remember about Danny's talk was the impact positive words had on his life. However, through his work with Desire Street, he learned that, unfortunately, the opposite was true for many people.

*Words can inspire. And words can
destroy. Choose yours well.*
—ROBIN SHARMA (SHARMA 2012)

Danny's story and message were so powerful they needed to be in this book. After some research, I came across a TEDx presentation Danny gave on December 10, 2021, at Pace Academy in Atlanta, Georgia. As Danny spoke, his voice, words, and body language brought back the emotions I remembered from the first presentation we had heard in Tampa years earlier.

Following his successful college and NFL career, a publishing company reached out to him, seeking to capitalize on his name and success. They suggested he outline key moments in his life along with any ideas he wanted to share.

Danny focused on his childhood. He remembered hearing an inner voice speaking to him during critical moments in his life. He shared some examples. Danny wanted to win the hundred-yard dash and earn a blue ribbon in first grade. "The voice inside my head said, 'Danny, you're so fast, you're so fast. You might be the fastest kid in your school. You might be the fastest kid in this whole county, state or country" (Wuerffel 2021). By the time race day came, he was so motivated. He ran the race and won, received the blue ribbon, and was happy.

In third grade, Danny recalled having to take a true-and-false test. He got to a question to which he didn't know the answer, so he decided to do some "research." "There was a girl to my left. She was really smart. I began to look at her paper, and remember this voice saying, 'Danny, you're a good kid, you're smart, you don't need to cheat, you're a good kid. So, I thought, I'm not going to do it'" (Wuerffel 2021).

Danny loved basketball. During his senior year in high school, the season was ending. His team qualified for the semifinals and would play against a team they had previously played. He recalled the team had a six-foot, six-inch-tall player who looked more like a football lineman. His height advantage meant he would get a lot of rebounds. Danny pointed out that the team with the most rebounds often wins the game.

His coach came up with an idea, a plan on how to play against this guy during the game. The coach told the team, "We'll play a box zone with four guys, have one person cover the big guy, and guard him all game." Everyone was excited; the coach was brilliant. He then told Danny, "You're the person who's going to cover the guy."

Immediately, Danny's face changed from excitement to worry. "No, no, no." Suddenly the plan didn't sound so brilliant anymore.

Before the game, Danny walked around his house, thinking, *Danny, you are so strong. You are the strongest guy out there. I don't care how big he is.* Feeling pumped up, he approached the bathroom. The door was closed. He thought, "Am I going to open it with a handle, or am I going to kick it down? Because I'm so strong" (Wuerffel 2021).

On game night, Danny's opponent walked onto the basketball court like he was in a World Wrestling Entertainment promo video. As he walked toward Danny, he got in his face and started talking smack, belittling him, and trying to get in his head.

Danny ignored the taunting and focused on the game plan. At the opening buzzer, reality hit. This smack-talking player *was* bigger and stronger than he had imagined. He remembers his inner voice's words of encouragement: *I'm the strongest one out there.* So Danny decided he needed leverage. He would have to get underneath this guy's center of gravity. With that advantage, Danny continually put his opponent in awkward positions that prevented him from playing well. At one point, he backed the guy up on the three-point line, and he got angry and used some colorful language that drew a technical foul from the referee. Danny made those free throws, and they went on to win the game. He credited his performance to his inner voice.

With those memories, he knew what his book would be about. He believed his inner voice resulted from how he talked to himself. If it worked for him, others might benefit from learning how to speak to themselves. He could teach them by writing a book.

While all these book discussions were taking place, Danny and his wife had their first child, a son, Jonah. His mom visited to help with her grandson. One morning he walked past his son's room and heard something; it was his mom. She was holding her grandson Jonah and telling him, "Jonah, you're such a good boy, you are so smart, you're strong and good." I've heard those words before.

A few minutes later, he heard his mom tell his son, "You are so strong, Jonah. You opened your eyelids. You're the strongest little three-day-old boy." His mother continued to speak affirming words to Jonah, praising him, "Jonah, you are such a good boy. You are so beautiful, strong, and special" (Wuerffel 2021).

*His mother's voice.*

For all those years, in all those difficult moments, the voice he had heard was that of his mother. He wept. It wasn't *his* voice in all those critical moments. The encouraging voices of affirmation belonged to his parents, extended family, teachers, coaches, and so many people who loved him.

He believed God worked through the people in his life to love him and ensure he felt valued. As his body language shifted and his voice lowered, Danny shared, "Before I had done anything good or bad, I was special. I was loved. I've been created in God's image, and I have worth because I'm a human being" (Wuerffel 2021).

After the TEDx Talk, someone caught up to him crying, using their sleeves to soak up the tears. Nearly out of breath, the guy told Danny how much his story moved him.

In a voice of compassion, Danny asked, "If you thought my story was good, why are you crying?"

Hesitating, the man told him, "I hear a lot of voices too, but they aren't always so positive."

I've been there as well. We all have. At some point in our lives, we heard discouraging words or worse.

However, another aspect of our relationships with people matters the most: being physically present and investing time.

*"Relationships take time and effort, and the best way to spell love is 'T-I-M-E.' The essence of love is not what we think or do or provide for others, but how much we give of ourselves."*

—RICK WARREN (WARREN 2002, 127)

When our children were young, Debbie put a framed placard of Dorothy Law Nolte's *Children Learn What They Live* on our family room wall. It reminded us that our words and actions have a lasting effect on our kids.

When children are criticized, ridiculed, or shamed, they tend to lash out at others. They become shy with people and feel guilty. Now emotionally depressed, those negative words become a repeating recording track in their minds.

On the other hand, when they heard, "we're proud of you," "great job on that project," and "thanks for helping with the chores," they felt valued, appreciated, and encouraged.

While our words can powerfully express our thoughts and ideas, the attitude or tone we use may speak louder than the actual words.

Growing up in my home, my sisters and I heard, "If you don't have anything nice to say, then don't say anything." As an adult, I would have benefited from remembering this advice. But unfortunately, for a time, my focus was on being *right* rather than loving and being considerate of the other person.

> *Generally speaking, fools think they are wise and 100 percent right—and the wise are aware of the incompleteness of their wisdom and their continued foolishness. Thus the foolish call out everyone and the wise do it sometimes but realize how different things may look in five years.*
>
> —TIM KELLER (KELLER 2022)

## BEHIND THE WORDS WE HEAR

Danny Wuerffel believed God spoke through his parents and other people in his life. The words he heard shaped the man he had become. As God's image bearers, we must use our words carefully.

As I was writing this chapter, I challenged myself to think about how many times I spoke words yesterday. And then I tried to remember something, anything I had said. It's not easy; try it. From the moment we get up until we go to bed, we talk at varying degrees.

Previously, we discussed social media's impact on communication. These platforms have reduced complicated issues and solutions to simple sound bites. We abbreviate and shorten the written word to the point of creating misunderstandings.

In her *Psychology Today* article "Our Words Matter," Mel Schwartz, LCSW, wrote, "Our words matter. The words we choose convey our thoughts and feelings. Aside from non-verbal communication, words are the heartbeat of our relationships. When we misuse our words or truncate our sentences to save time, we dishonor ourselves and our relationships" (Schwartz 2019).

What narrative voice are you hearing? Is it helpful or harmful? What narrative are our words creating in the hearts and minds of the people in our lives? What and whose words are you listening to and allowing to take root in your heart and mind?

Like this book you are reading, each of us is being "read." Our words, actions, attitudes, and body language all say something. I want mine to be encouraging and inspiring.

I read a good book, *Words That Work: It's Not What You Say, It's What People Hear*, written by Dr. Frank Luntz. He spotlighted how we use words and how the words we choose convey a message. Words can make people feel something, and they have consequences. In the first chapter, Frank recalled something Warren Beatty told him:

> *"People will forget what you say but not how you made them feel"*
> —WARREN BEATTY (LUNTZ 2007, 18)

I want to make people feel welcomed and valued. I want my words to be memorable so that when they are replayed in their minds, they encourage and inspire them. Why? Danny Wuerffel answered that as he closed his TED Talk,

Are you paying attention to that voice that's in your head? Is it true? Is it a lie? Is it helpful? Is it not? Where does it come from? Are you paying attention? And most importantly, like my mom, we all can help shape that voice in someone else.

So, whether you're holding an infant in a nursery or whether you're walking out of a TEDx Talk and smiling at someone, whatever it is, we have the opportunity to help shape that voice because the voice that's on the inside determines so much of who we are. (Wuerffel 2021)

## REFLECTIONS

Danny's words struck a nerve. I reflected on my past conversations—specifically, those with Debbie. Many could have gone better. Unfortunately, too many ended poorly. I believe Frank Luntz's book title hit the nail on the head: it's not what you say; it's what people hear. When speaking, I needed to be clear so what I *intended* to say *is* what other people hear.

I want my words to encourage people and inspire hope. A correction would come gentler, more loving, and more compassionate if required. For this to be true, my words must become part of the internal fabric of who I am—my heart and character.

To do this, I decided to take a brief pause and say a quick prayer to listen actively, understand what was said, and respond appropriately.

We've all experienced "brief pauses." For example, live broadcasting on TV or radio has brief broadcast delays intended to prevent inappropriate or unacceptable words from being heard by listeners.

In her book, *A Good Day at School: Take Charge of Emotions So Your Child Can Find Happiness,* Kat Mulvaney offers valuable principles for parents. Including how to understand children's emotions and manage volatility to ensure mutual health in the parent-child relationship. She opened her chapter "The New You" with the following quote:

Speak to your children as if they are the wisest, kindest, most beautiful and magical humans on earth, for what they believe is what they will become. —Brook Hampton (Mulvaney 2020)

I believe Danny Wuerffel would agree. This was the essence of how his mother spoke in his life. I would have appreciated this understanding early in our childrearing days.

Speaking affirming words is a choice. It requires planning and educating ourselves to know and understand how to parent as our children mature. They grow physically and emotionally in various phases. We need to know those phases to give our kids the best chance of becoming well-adjusted adults.

To learn more, I found these two books helpful: *It's Just a Phase So Don't Miss It: Why Every Life Stage of a Kid Matters* by Reggie Joiner and Kristen Ivy, and *Cure for the Common Life: Living in Your Sweet Spot* by Max Lucado.

Being a proactive and informed parent will reduce relational tension and stress in your home.

I will leave you with these thoughts. What are the words you are speaking? What are people hearing? Are they worth remembering? How did you make them feel?

And most importantly, is it more important for you to *be right* or right with others? In other words, as my family has heard me say often, conversations don't have to be like tennis matches with all the back and forth until someone loses.

Everyone loses when our words are not encouraging or helpful.

# CHAPTER 8

# LISTENING SETBACKS

*When God wants to make a mushroom, he takes*
*six hours. When God wants to make an oak tree, he*
*takes 60 years. The question is: Do you want*
*your life to be a mushroom or an oak tree?*

—RICK WARREN

Everything in this life has a beginning, a starting point. You and I had a beginning—the day we were born. From that moment forward, we begin a process that involves hearing, seeing, touching, tasting, and smelling. These senses allow us to experience the world and our environments.

We have already discussed the importance listening plays in developing healthy relationships with the people in our lives. We've talked about learning to listen and looked at Danny Wuerffel's powerful story, where he would hear an inner voice speaking to him in critical moments in his life. But what is our inner voice?

Some people describe their inner voice as an internal monologue—the conversations we have with ourselves. For example, on the way to the grocery store, I could hear, *Don't forget to get the milk and eggs.* I'm expecting my "inner voice" to remind me. Sometimes it does. Other times, I picked up items that caught my attention but that we didn't need.

Others might describe their inner voice as their conscience alerting them in specific situations about right and wrong or good versus bad.

As with all prompts from our inner voice, we can either pay attention or ignore them.

### SPIRITUAL LISTENING BEGINS WITH AN INTERNAL STIRRING

You've likely experienced some form of internal stirring. I have. I just didn't have a name for it. It's unsettling in a situation or conversation, and you feel a nudge or prompting.

Remember that poking I was feeling during the services at First Baptist in Orlando? The emotional reactions I had to the sermons? At times it felt like a more pronounced nudge. Sometimes I just felt unsettled. Something was stirring inside. What did this all mean?

I now know who the inner voice belongs to. Unlike self-speak—telling myself what I want to hear—this inner voice offers guidance, truth, insight, wisdom, and warnings.

*This inner voice is the most important and powerful voice we can listen to. It is the voice of God inviting you and me to come and see, to come and learn.*

Learning to listen and obey would take time and a willingness to pay attention to the promptings. It takes time to know how to respond and what action to take. For me, learning to tune in involved a lot of trial and error. I wanted to understand and take the appropriate action—but I struggled and still do.

When we pray, we speak to God, and that's true. But more importantly, He speaks to us when we read our Bibles.

I've learned, sometimes the hard way, that it is far more critical to listen to what God is saying over any other voices, including my own. He knows everything about me and is committed to maturing you and me so that we reflect His image and character.

But there is a big *but*. We need to cooperate. Reading the Bible provides the foundation on which to build our lives. It is essential to transforming into a better version of ourselves. God's work within us may seem cryptic or indistinct initially. But we learn valuable skills over time as we read, listen, and act. The more we practice, the more tuned in we become. The result will be less static. Tuning out the other voices in our lives allows us to tune in to hear God's voice.

Do you remember the old radios with tuning dials? We had to turn the dial back and forth to get a clear signal. Fortunately, we don't have to do that anymore, but unfortunately, it is still part of how we seek to hear God speaking to us. Learning to listen and obey God is like adjusting the tuning dial. The more we respond immediately, the clearer and more consistently we hear His voice. However, it is harder to hear Him when we ignore or delay responding. It can also be painful.

Pastor Rick Warren described the Holy Spirit:

*Only the Holy Spirit has the power to make the changes God wants to make in your life. Mention the power of the Holy Spirit, and many people think of miraculous demonstrations or intense emotions. But usually, the Holy Spirit releases his power in your*

*life in quiet, unassuming ways that you aren't even*
*aware of. He often nudges you with "a gentle whisper*
—RICK WARREN (WARREN 2012, 174)

You and I cannot create change within ourselves on our own. We have all made New Year's resolutions we didn't keep. Best intentions or willpower are generally not going to produce desired results.

We need power and strength we don't have, which will be found only by trusting God with our lives and allowing Him to do what we cannot. His Spirit is the strength, power, and wisdom we can count on if we choose to cooperate.

As we cooperate, we also must be patient. Transforming our lives will be a slow process. Many of us have past habits and pain packed into us, and unpacking, if done correctly, will take time.

I want to be like an oak tree, firmly and strongly planted and able to withstand the storms of life. And storms come in various shapes, sizes, and situations. They also come from the people in our lives.

## LISTENING PREVENTS SERIOUS INJURY

*One way to define wisdom is the ability to see, into*
*the future, the consequences of your choices in the*
*present. That ability can give you a completely different*
*perspective on what the future might look like.*
—ANDY ANDREWS (ANDREWS 2009, 65)

While living in Florida, one of our neighbors, Bruce Uhler, was offered an opportunity to work in his company's headquarters in Nybro, Sweden. By the time they had to move, one of the things they couldn't take care of was selling their minivan. I agreed to help them.

We lived at the end of a cul-de-sac. Our home sat on a property called a flag lot. The driveway was much longer than our neighbors. All our kids had driver's licenses and cars. On many days we had to juggle moving four to five cars. In addition, Margo and Bruce's 2006 Nissan van was parked in the driveway.

I served as an usher during our church's Saturday evening service. Debbie and I were getting ready to leave one afternoon, and I had to move some cars to get to our Highlander. As I approached Uhler's van to move it, my inner voice clearly said, *Just take the van.* My first response was no, it's not my van, even though the Uhlers told us to use it anytime until it was sold. However, the prompt was clear, so I got into the driver's seat and waited for Debbie. She gave the what's-up shrug, walking to the car. I said, "Let's just take the van. It's easier than moving cars." So off we went to church.

After the service was over, it was dark as we headed home. After exiting at Lake Mary Boulevard, we turned right, heading south of Lake Emma Road. We are only two miles from home. *Everything is good; no problems.* We approach a red light and stop. No car in front of us. Suddenly, I hear a loud motorcycle coming from behind us. In a split second, *kaboom*—we're hit. Jolted forward. I immediately turned to Debbie to make sure she was okay.

Getting out of the van, a guy was on the ground, and the front wheel of his motorcycle was wedged underneath the van's rear bumper. He was screaming someone's name. It was his passenger. She had been thrown to the side of the road. Being a nurse, Debbie checked the driver and passenger. I called 911.

In those frantic minutes, another guy—the driver of the car that hit the motorcycle—appeared visibly upset and asked if everyone was okay.

Eventually, the police arrived, along with the paramedics. The motorcycle driver looked banged up but seemed okay. However, they took his passenger to the local hospital.

I could hear the sheriff's officer talking to the car's driver. He remembered dropping something, and after picking it up, he looked up and hit the motorcycle.

After the sheriff's officer checked to be sure everyone was okay, he turned to me and said, "I need to see your driver's license and vehicle registration."

I entered the passenger door and opened the glove box to retrieve the vehicle registration. *This isn't my van. I hope this doesn't become a problem.* "Here you go, officer. This van isn't mine. It belongs to our neighbors who moved to Sweden. I'm helping them sell it." *Hoping to diffuse any potential issues.*

The officer asked, "What kind of car do you own?

"A 2004 Toyota Highlander," I replied.

"You all are very lucky," the officer said in an emotional voice. "If you had been driving the Highlander, this accident might have been much worse."

"Why?" I replied.

"Because the Highland bumper sits much higher than the van. The gas tank is partially exposed. The impact force on the motorcycle would have sent it like a projectile under the bumper. The gas tank could have exploded," the officer said with confidence, as though he had experienced that kind of accident.

"Unbelievable," I said. "I was hesitant taking the van since it wasn't mine, but at the last minute...I decided to drive it."

"It's a good thing you did," the officer said as he walked toward the other driver.

Still shaken by the accident and realizing it could have been much worse, I looked up. *Thank you, Lord! Thank you for prompting me to take the van.* At that moment, relief and gratitude washed over me. I was thankful I listened and didn't ignore the Spirit's prompting.

But that wasn't the end of the story. I emailed Bruce asking him to call as soon as possible. When we talked, he and Margo couldn't care less about the van. They were glad we were not injured and that nobody else was seriously hurt. The insurance company totaled the car, and when they told me how much the amount would be, it was $1,500 more than the price the Uhlers were asking for the van. Unbelievable!

I learned a valuable lesson that day. Pay attention to and listen to God's prompts. We didn't escape the accident, but no one was seriously injured. It could have been worse if I had ignored God's voice. Unfortunately, that embedded memory didn't guarantee I would listen and obey every time.

## NOT LISTENING ENDS WITH AN INJURY

*One of the main reasons that we trust God too little is because we trust our own wisdom too much. We think we know far better than God how our lives should go and what will make us happy.*
—TIM KELLER (KELLER 2021)

As we have discussed, we have a choice to listen or to ignore. I enjoyed living in Florida because of the ability to be outdoors all year. One of my favorite activities was rollerblading. I'd been skating since 1995 when we lived in New Jersey. One of my routines was taking my son Nicholas's dog Reese out so she could run while I skated. We had wide, paved walking trails throughout the county. One of the trailheads was about two blocks from our community

The week before our daughter Morgan's high school senior prom in May 2008, I decided to stop at the flagpole at Lake Mary High School and pray for the students and teachers for a safe prom. This route took me off the paved trails and onto local sidewalks. No big deal. I've skated on sidewalks before. However, not with Reese alongside me. I committed to doing this every day, including Saturday, the day of the prom.

I skated the same route without any issues. Saturday morning arrived—the last day of this ritual, the big day, and the final opportunity to pray over the prom. Reese and I took off just like every other day. Coming off the trail, I'm heading east on Lake Way Road toward Longwood Lake Mary Road and the high school.

As I approached the intersection of Lake Park Drive, that quiet voice said, "You might want to turn around and go back the other way." I shook my head as if to say, *What was that about?* I ignored the prompt. I was determined to pray at the flagpole that morning, period. I was approaching Longwood Lake Mary Road, and I heard the same warning, only louder. I ignored the inner voice a second time.

As I turned the corner heading south on Longwood Lake Mary Road, I saw a group of eight female joggers coming toward me. Panic set in. Get the image here: I'm on rollerblades, holding a seventy-pound boxer German shepherd mix dog on a leash on a sidewalk. My heart was pounding. The runners all moved to the grass and went around Reese and me. *Whew, crisis averted*, I thought. We continued toward Lake Mary High School. I approached a curve on the sidewalk that went around a clump of trees hiding the view on the other side.

Reese and I were now coming around the trees, and suddenly, a lone jogger was in front of us.

To this day, I have no idea what happened. For some reason, Reese started barking, pulling, and going crazy. In an instant, I was pulled down and slammed to the ground. I hit my chin and face. I looked up and heard this woman yelling at me to get control of the dog, still barking and lunging for her. *Really?* I just looked at her, dazed and silent. She finally started jogging away. I'm lying on the ground, thinking, *What in the hell just happened?* As I checked myself out, my knee was in severe pain with cuts, scraps, and blood, as were my left wrist, chin, and lip.

I got up slowly. My knee had now ballooned in size. I could barely flex it. *Skating home is going to be a challenge. Should I call Debbie for a ride?* Instantly, I realized, *Why didn't I listen to the warning?* But I didn't. Why? Because I had plans, and nothing would stop me. Now humbled, I'm only a few hundred feet from the high school. I made my way to the flagpole and ended my prayer by apologizing to God for not listening and asking for forgiveness. The consequences of not listening were going to be painful for a while.

Arriving home, Debbie saw me and wanted to know what had happened. I looked pretty beat up. As I cleaned up, looking at myself in the mirror, I noticed a red rash mark on my right shoulder and one on my left wrist. At that moment, I said to God, "Please, please do not heal these wounds on my left wrist and my right shoulder. I want those scars to be a reminder to listen!" As I write this, both scars remain and have served as reminders to listen to His voice, but not consistently.

I thought of that incident many times. The irony is hard to miss. I sought God in prayer to watch over and protect everyone involved in the prom. I expected Him to hear me.

And on the other hand, I heard Him provide a clear warning to protect me. But I didn't listen. Actually, that's not true. I decided to ignore Him. Go figure.

## MY PLANS OR GOD'S PLAN

After we moved to Lake Mary, my stepmother Madeleine mentioned her Uncle Harry lived in Orlando alone. His wife had died many years earlier. Harry was a WWII vet who was legally blind due to macular degeneration. He could see well enough to live independently. But had given up his driver's license years earlier. I began to help Harry, we moved him to an assisted living facility, and he became a member of our family.

One day, Harry had a couple of medical appointments. I was a bit stressed because I was in the middle of a couple of projects. On this day, I just wanted to get in and out of the doctor's office and get back to work.

I arrived early to pick Harry up. As I walked into the facility, a woman sat by herself in the screened porch area. I didn't recognize her and figured she was new. "Good morning. How are you today?" No facial expression or response.

As I left with Harry, the woman was still sitting in the same chair. "Have a great day!" I said.

Harry and I returned a few hours later. We entered the screened porch, and guess what? Yep, the woman hadn't moved. *Geez, what's up with her?* For the third time, I said, "Hi, how are you?" Again, no response.

With Harry settled back in his room, I quickly left for home. As I exited the building through the screened porch, I said, "Goodbye. Have a great day." No response. My hand touched the handle on the screen door, ready to walk out, and I heard the Spirit clearly: *Go back and talk to that woman.*

*Nope, gotta go. I don't have time for this.* I kept walking to my car.

As I put the key in the car door, I heard again, only louder: *Go back and talk to that woman.* Once again, I ignored the clear prompt. I've got work to do.

With the key in the ignition, I turned the car on. One more time, God's voice spoke, but much louder: *Go back and talk to that woman!*

Exasperated, I turned the car off. I looked up and said, "Alright, alright already. I'll go talk to that woman."

Listening does involve setbacks. Why? Because I wanted to do what I had planned on doing! It makes no sense. I heard the voice of God, yet I was not open to being interrupted. I know better; my response should always be yes! Without hesitation or questioning.

What's crazy is I taught a Bible study in *this* facility while attending a men's Bible class and teaching in the children's program. And at that moment, I completely ignored the voice of God. *Self*-interests exerted themselves.

I walked into the screened porch and sat down next to the woman. She was still expressionless. I placed my right hand on her left knee and simply said, "Is there something I could pray for you about?" Immediately, she started to cry. I listened this time. Over the next hour or so, she told me her name, Ruby, and that her family had put her in the facility. She didn't want to be there. I encouraged her, telling her the facility, staff, and residents were great and that she'd settle in soon.

Ruby shared a little about herself. Finally, she was relaxed and calm and became a bit chatty. I asked if she wanted a cup of coffee. She told me she didn't drink coffee and preferred tea.

I told her about Harry and that it took a few weeks for him to adjust to new routines. But he flourished participating in the activities offered and bus trip outings. As we closed our time together, I invited Ruby to our next Bible study. "You're going to meet some nice people."

Leaving this time, I felt less stressed and at peace. I was relieved I went back and talked to "that woman." But I was frustrated, once again, that I struggled with listening and obeying God. What was I thinking? What arrogance believing my plans were more important than doing what God asked me to do? As I'm writing this, the irony is clear. Ruby ignored me four times, I ignored God twice, and then I reluctantly did what He asked the third time.

On my way home, I stopped by our Target and purchased a Mr. Coffee Tea Maker and various teas to bring to Ruby the next day. Her room was only a few doors away from Harry's. When I presented her with the tea maker, her face lit up. It was priceless. She got involved with the Bible study group and began participating in various activities.

I stopped by most days and checked in on her. One day, Inez, the activities director, called to let me know Ruby was in South Seminole hospital. It was ten minutes from our home, and Debbie worked there.

It was a Saturday on Easter weekend. We had family and friends coming in for the weekend, so I got busy and forgot to go and see Ruby. Easter evening, Debbie said she would check in on her when she went to work on Monday. Unfortunately, I got the call early Monday morning that she had passed away.

I was sad I didn't get to see Ruby before she passed, but I rejoiced, knowing she was now in the arms of Jesus. One day I expect to see her when I arrive in heaven.

That morning, I apologized to God again for almost missing the opportunity He arranged to make a difference in Ruby's life. I had peace knowing that, though reluctant at first, I was able to show her love and bring joy and some happiness during her last seven weeks on earth.

**REFLECTIONS**

*You know you are maturing when you begin to see the hand of God in the random, baffling, and seemingly pointless circumstances of life.*
—RICK WARREN (WARREN 2002, 199)

These stories are only a few of many instances of living in the tension and struggle between doing what we want to do and ignoring God's prompts rather than doing what He asks. We have no idea what is on the other side of our obedience or disobedience.

However, in hindsight, it was obvious. Listening and taking the van prevented serious injury to Debbie, me, the motorcycle driver, and his passenger.

Not listening while rollerblading led to ignoring God's warning of danger ahead and an injury that took weeks to resolve.

And despite reluctantly letting go of my plans and allowing God to control my calendar, Ruby was blessed. Her final days were in peace and joy. God demonstrated amazing grace and patience with me.

And just as I asked for those scars to remain with me as reminders to listen, I wanted these stories to serve as anchor moments of God's presence in my life. Those memories reminded me that when the next warning or opportunity comes, my answer is yes, no matter what God asks.

Listening to and obeying the voice of God is not easy. It should be. Think about it. God is the creator of the universe.

He knows the past, present, and future—mine and yours. The wisest decision we can make is to respond to His voice and counsel immediately. Period. Why? Because He always has our best interest in mind, even when we don't. He knows the future. We don't. It's just foolish to choose our way over His.

Partial obedience is disobedience. I don't want to be disobeying God.

In God's providence, while writing this chapter, I am attending the BSF Men's group in Orlando virtually. We just began the study of the Kingdom Divided. In his lecture for lesson four (1 Kings 15:25–18:46), Ed Wood, our teaching leader, said:

*God lets us choose what we want, but we don't get to choose what the consequences will be.*

Those words summed up these stories perfectly.

*Lord, may my answer always be yes, whatever you ask. Give me the courage to act immediately.*

I wish I could say this is always true, but I'm a work in progress. I am comforted by the apostle Paul's words to followers of Jesus in Philippi: "And I am certain that God, who began the good work within you, will continue his work until it is finally finished on the day when Christ Jesus returns" (Philippians 1:6, NLT).

PART FOUR

# FINDING HOPE

CHAPTER 9

# IN THE BIBLE

*Someone has said that there are four things necessary in studying the Bible: Admit, submit, commit and transmit.*

—DWIGHT L. MOODY

Bad church experiences—we've all had them. It calls "religion" into question. We observe people who claim to be "religious" living their lives like everybody else, and sometimes worse. We all know people who are hypocrites. As I've shared before, that includes me. We all want to be "read" well. We sand off the rough edges and seek to hide our blemishes behind a thin veneer of painted perfection.

But what do bad experiences with people or churches have to do with God? Nothing! Jesus had much to say about the religious leaders of His day—mostly negative. He would agree with you walking away from those situations and then invite you to "follow" Him. How? By reading His story.

## THE BEST-SELLING BOOK

Many people have heard about the Bible and have an opinion, pro or con. This is true regardless of whether they have read it. In the article "10 surprising facts about the Bible,"

Chanshi Chibwe cited the *Guinness Book of World Records,* saying more than five billion copies have been purchased since 1851. Astonishingly, one hundred million Bibles are sold every year (Chibwe 2019).

Chanshi shared something interesting but not surprising: according to the American Bible Society study in 2017, women are 20 percent more likely to read the Bible than men. I have previously discussed that BSF was a significant part of my personal and spiritual growth. It was founded as a women's Bible study in 1959, with men's classes added many years later.

In addition to the many Bible versions available in print form, I enjoy the access to the digital versions available through the YouVersion Bible app. According to their website, in November 2021, the app surpassed five hundred million unique installs from users worldwide. The YouVersion community has completed 1.4 billion Bible Plan days. Bible engagement continues to rise as people seek information to understand how they fit in God's story but also to learn lessons that can be applied in their lives.

I have come to believe humans are good at hiding the truth from themselves. We want to be liked. To be highly thought of. If you and I were to write our life story, we would be the heroes. We would only write flattering things about ourselves. And for those reasons, I believe that truly makes one of the strongest arguments for the authenticity and accuracy of the Bible. Not convinced? You will be after you begin to read it for yourself.

The Bible presents the people and cultures in brutal honesty. Hearts and minds are exposed for all to see and read. Every blemish, mistake, and action, even those things done or thought in secret, have been placed under a microscope and a floodlight. Various writers present themselves and others in unflattering and compromising situations. Why? So you and I can relate. Because the truth is, nothing about you and me is hidden from God. He knows everything about us. D.L. Moody is right. Our response must be, "admit, submit, commit, and transmit."

Ed Wood, the teaching leader in the Orlando Evening Men's BSF class, said something I have never forgotten:

*Imagine the day you are called to account for your life. All your family and friends are sitting in a theater waiting to watch the movie of your life. You're excited. Thinking about the highlight showreel everyone is going to see. But to your surprise, God tells the audience they are going to watch the movie of your life that played out in your heart and mind—the hidden, unseen life. Exposing your true motives. What was only known to you and God.*

Gulp.

### READING THE BIBLE

God ensured you and I have access to His Story—unvarnished. Our story is inferred and embedded in the lives, people, and cultures of hundreds of stories over thousands of years. Why? So in every generation—past, present, and future—we can identify basic human characteristics that are always true. God wants our hearts and souls aligned with His. The only way to authentic transformation is from the inside out, not the outside in.

The challenge with following culture's preferences is that they generally ignore God's principles for right living—with Him and each other. Preferences are interpreted by people generally for their benefit and often at the expense of others.

Preferences can't serve as anchors because they are movable. The author of the book *Judges* wrote about the nation of Israel's continual cycle of disobedience due to their preferences. They repeatedly ignored God's principles and commands. However, in His grace, they were delivered from their folly, time after time. The last sentence punctuated the state of the nation and culture. "In those days Israel had no king; all the people did whatever seemed right in their own eyes" (Judges 21:25, NLT). Has anything changed?

Dwight L. Moody's formal education ended in the fifth grade. He had confident hope in God. His academic and spiritual contribution to the world continues through the Moody Bible Institute in Chicago. He wrote, "Where one man reads the Bible, a hundred read you and me" (Moody 2020).

What will they read?

Though Moody wrote that quote in the 1800s, it remains relevant today. He challenged his audience and you and me with a question: What's the point of listening to sermons if the good news you hear about doesn't make a difference in your life? If what we believe is not observed in how we live, no one will be drawn to want to know more about God. Moody said something profound: "Some little act of kindness will perhaps do more to influence them than any number of long sermons" (Moody 2020).

I shared how reading the Bible and applying what I learned in practical ways profoundly impacted my life. And honestly, that's an understatement. So, I thought some background would be helpful.

When I first began reading *Every Man's Bible* in 2006, I did a flyover by thumbing through all the books and chapters. It was a bit overwhelming. It appeared complex. I couldn't grasp how all of it was connected.

I struggled with the concept of an all-knowing, all-powerful, good God. A God who allows pain and suffering in the world. How could God possibly relate to humanity? After all, I believed he was distant from us, way up in heaven, just looking down on everything in this world. The church I was raised in presented God as divine and otherworldly. But he was also to be feared. He would pronounce judgment for my wrongdoing. It was tough to believe and understand how to know God—if that was even possible.

### UNDERSTANDING PAIN

If you're in a place of pain, you're not alone. In my dark days, I read *Where Is God When It Hurts?* Philip Yancey tackled this huge topic by sharing insights from the Bible and his personal experience. In the well-researched chapter on hope, Philip discussed the contributions of the Christian faith on the topic. He wrote, "The Christian believes that, no matter how bleak things look at the present, something good really does lie ahead" (Yancey 1990, 217).

During my study of Romans, Paul's words written two thousand years ago to struggling followers of Jesus in Rome offered comfort and hope. They are paraphrased as follows: "Through our Lord Jesus Christ, we have obtained access by faith into this grace in which we stand, and we rejoice in hope of the glory of God. Not only that, but we rejoice in our sufferings, knowing that suffering produces endurance and endurance produces character, and character produces hope, and hope does not put us to shame, because God's love has been poured out into our hearts through the Holy Spirit who has been given to us" (Romans 5:1-5, ESV).

My breakthrough moment occurred in the eighth chapter of Romans. Paul wrote:

*Yet what we suffer now is nothing compared to the glory he will reveal to us later. And the Holy Spirit helps us in our weakness. For example, we don't know what God wants us to pray for. But the Holy Spirit prays for us with groanings that cannot be expressed in words. And the Father who knows all hearts knows what the Spirit is saying, for the Spirit pleads for us believers in harmony with God's own will. And we know that God causes everything to work together for the good of those who love God and are called according to his purpose for them* (ROMANS 8:18,26-28 NLT).

After months of reading and studying Romans in the Bible, I finally saw the connection. Jesus is my Savior and Lord. I have His Spirit living in me. I am not alone. He walks with me through every situation, every trial, and every test. I have confident hope.

## RESISTING READING THE BIBLE

In our lives, we've all experienced *firsts*. Our first day of elementary school, middle school, and high school. Our first day of working, or the first day in a new career. How about our first dates? Or that first day after you're married. Many *firsts* include anxiety and fear of the unknown. Why? Well, we've never been there before. Every new event, experience, or encounter had a first time, a beginning. In every case, we had to learn academically, professionally, and relationally for the first time. And as we invested our time, it got easier to understand or relate. Our faith journeys will include many firsts, including reading the Bible.

Generally, we don't approach our firsts with a know-it-all attitude. We go in open-hearted, open-minded, and open-handed.

So, it's curious that we begin with resistance when it comes to our faith journey or our first time reading the Bible. We hold onto preconceived notions and ideas of what "we" think it should be.

When I became a teaching leader for the Richmond, Virginia, evening men's class, I would often say to our guys, "We study and wrestle with a lot of mysteries, difficult passages, and challenging concepts. We will not always agree. So, I'd like to suggest we focus on what we know to be true and trustworthy rather than what is unexplainable. Only the Holy Spirit can help us understand God's word and what it means to you and me."

My own experience confirms this. In the beginning, I struggled to understand what I was reading, let alone what I was to do with what I was reading. However, I committed to consistently reading the Bible. I asked the Holy Spirit to help me understand and apply what I had learned.

Every person reading the Bible is on a unique and personal journey. We are rarely in the same place at the same time, and that's okay. God customizes our learning to what we can handle and absorb. Think of it like building a brick home. With a solid, level foundation, the first brick is a cornerstone. Only over time do you have a solid structure able to resist the weather and storms that will come. We wouldn't take shortcuts building our homes. We need to make the same commitment, perseverance, and investment of time in Bible study.

One of my favorite ministries is Starting Point. I've been a facilitator for many years. We create safe conversational environments for people who are "seekers, starters, or returners." Seekers are people curious about faith, exploring "religion," or just want information about God, the Bible, and Jesus. Starters are those who have taken their next step in learning and are growing relationally with Jesus. Returners are folks raised in the church but who walked away. Now they want to reset their faith as adults. In our first Starting Point group meeting, we clarify:

> *The starting point for the Christian faith is a question: Who is Jesus? And The Christian faith isn't about what Jesus said before he died. It's about what happened after he died: he rose from the dead* (STANLEY 2014, 18).

Early in my journey, I read Philip Yancey's *The Bible Jesus Read*. The title intrigued me. In the opening pages, he addresses an important objection:

> *The Old Testament portrays the world as it is, no holds barred. In its pages you will find passionate stories of love and hate, blood-chilling stories of rape and dismemberment, matter-of-fact accounts of trafficking in slaves, honest tales of the high honor and cruel treachery of war. Nothing is neat and orderly. Spoiled brats like Solomon and Samson get supernatural gifts; a truly good man like Job gets catastrophe.* (YANCEY 1999, 11).

Yancey followed with an interesting perspective by Kathleen Norris. In her book *Amazing Grace,* she acknowledged people generally feel something is missing in their lives. They have a desire for something without knowing exactly what it is. Often it is of a spiritual nature, a desire to be in a community of faith. However, after trying to read the Bible, "[t]hey end up throwing it across the room" (Yancey 1999, 12).

Throwing the Bible expresses a raw and honest frustration that is part of how our story intersects with God's as He openly shares in its pages. The Bible creates an inherent tension as we see aspects of ourselves in the people and situations we read about. And rather than honestly facing the truth about us, we dismiss the Bible as being "negative, vengeful, and violent."

Kathleen said something profound:

*I can only hope that they are rejecting the violence-as-entertainment of movies and television on the same grounds, and that they say a prayer every time they pick up a daily newspaper or turn on CNN. In the context of real life, the Bible seems refreshingly whole, an honest reflection on humanity in relation to the sacred and the profane. I can't learn enough about it, but I also have to trust what little I know, and proceed, in faith, to seek God there.* (YANCEY 1999, 12).

When Paul wrote his second letter to his protege Timothy, Paul reminded him, "All Scripture is inspired by God and is useful to teach us what is true and to make us realize what is wrong in our lives. It corrects us when we are wrong and teaches us to do what is right. God uses it to prepare and equip his people to do every good work" (2 Timothy 3:16-17, NLT).

Philip Yancey made a statement I completely agree with:

*A warning: it may prove dangerous to get involved with the Bible. You approach it with a series of questions, and*

*as you enter it you find the questions turned back upon you.*
*King David got swept up in a story by the prophet Nathan*
*and leaped to his feet indignant—only to learn the barbed*
*story concerned himself* (YANCEY 1999, 13-14).

## REFLECTIONS

Everyone who reads the Bible and seeks to know God will come
face to face and heart to heart with the truth about their lives.
That is the point, and that is a good thing. It has been said
the Bible is the only book we read that reads us. After sixteen
years, I can say with certainty that it is true. In my experience,
at different moments, I felt like I was reading about myself in
the passages I was reading and studying.

Philip Yancey quoted Thomas Merton's words from *Open-ing the Bible*:

> *There is, in a word, nothing comfortable about the Bible—*
> *until we manage to get so used to it that we make it com-*
> *fortable for ourselves...Have we ceased to question the book*
> *and be questioned by it? Have we ceased to fight it? Then*
> *perhaps our reading is no longer serious* (YANCEY 1999, 14).

A natural tension is created when we read passages. As
we investigate through commentaries, we wrestle with our
understanding of what God has said. This is where the rubber meets the road—seeing ourselves in the passages. Are we
going to choose God's principles or our preferences? That was
my awakening when reading Jesus' words about adultery; I
learned it was a matter of my heart. Jesus was clear: where and
on what we fix our hearts and minds are equally as important
as our actions.

That, I believe, is the beauty of the Bible. Unlike any other book, it speaks to us in such a way that our hearts, souls, and minds are pricked or unsettled. It causes us to get real and honest with ourselves. If we truly want life transformation, we will listen to what is being called to mind and take the appropriate corrective actions.

> *The important thing is not to stop questioning. Curiosity has its own reason for existing. One cannot help but be in awe when he contemplates the mysteries of eternity, of life, of the marvelous structure of reality. It is enough if one tries merely to comprehend a little of this mystery every day. Never lose a holy curiosity...Don't stop to marvel.*
>
> —ALBERT EINSTEIN (MILLER 1955, 64)

As we close our time together, I will remind us that the only person ever to predict their own death and resurrection and pull it off was Jesus of Nazareth. Back to the most important question everyone needs to answer – who is Jesus to you? If you want to know Jesus, read what those who were closest to him wrote. To see and hear words come alive, I would highly recommend The Chosen, a multi-season show about the life of Jesus – as you watch Him interact with men, women, and children, you will want to have a personal relationship with Him.

We would be wise to learn as much as possible about what He said about the Jewish scriptures, Himself, God, and humanity. Start reading your Bible, and be amazed by how it speaks to you. You recall from the introduction that John said, "Jesus did many other miraculous signs in the presence of his followers which are not recorded in this book. *But*, these are written so that *you* may *believe* that Jesus is the Christ, the Son of God. *Then* by believing, you may have life through His name" (John 20:30–31, NCV).

For additional information about Starting Point, visit the website. It is a great place to find resources to help you understand faith. Self-study plans are available. Additional resources can be found by searching the internet, podcasts, and social media. Many churches, Bible colleges, and seminary programs are now offering free online courses.

Everyone is on a personal journey, and resources to grow are available for every stage along the way.

We could not possibly cover all that needs to be said about the Bible in one chapter. However, let John's words be your big idea, and the words of Albert Einstein be your invitation to start.

Be holy curious!

# CHAPTER 10

# IN A PENDANT

*To be a child of God means access. We know God is
attentively listening to us and watching us. Conversation
with God leads to an encounter with God.*

—TIMOTHY KELLER

## WALKING AND TALKING WITH GOD

On Valentine's Day 2005, I was on the phone in my home
office. My son, Nicholas, walked in the front door with a puppy.
Everyone was excited except me. One hand on the phone, and
the other gesturing, "no way," I shook my head no.

Despite protesting this black-and-brown puppy's arrival,
the family decided she would stay, as you already guessed
from learning about my skating accident earlier. It didn't take
the kids long to come up with a name: Reese. They reasoned
her colors reminded them of Reese's peanut butter cups. We
all grew to enjoy having Reese as part of the family. She was
a source of companionship. In eleven months, she would also
provide vitally needed comfort.

I have always been an avid walker, being outdoors alone
with my thoughts. Over the years, I would use that time to

listen to podcasts and audiobooks. However, after April 10, 2006, those walks would include time just talking to God. Sharing or screaming what was rattling inside my mind. Fears, doubts, concerns, frustrations. Yet always grateful for what He was doing in my life.

In a later chapter, I'll share how those walks and talks with God often included opportunities to share my hope with others. And yet, the elusive thing I hoped for remained: finding Jennifer. For a long time, my prayer was, "Lord, I ask You to give me a supernatural revelation of where Jennifer is so I can go and get her and bring her home."

We were now approaching the end of 2007. We were no closer to answers on Jennifer's whereabouts. So, I waited. Praying, hoping for an answer, any answer. It was frustrating.

## FASTING

Our pastor announced he would encourage the entire congregation to consider beginning the 2008 new year with a fast. The church provided resources to read. Pastor David explained we could "fast" in a number of ways, but the goal was to sacrifice something in our lives to spend more focused time with God.

My ears perked up. I realized this might be a great way to break the log jam I felt about Jennifer's case. Spending quality time with God would help me grow in my relationship with Him. On the drive home, I remembered my dad and I had attended a men's conference in Lincroft, New Jersey, during the summer. On a break, we visited various vendors. One had an extensive collection of books. As I looked over the table, a title caught my attention. It was a book by Bill Bright called *The Transforming Power of Fasting and Prayer*. I decided to buy it for no reason or purpose. But now, I had a reason, so I started reading the book. Chapter two was titled "Fasting Transforms Us to Transform the World." Bill Bright said:

> *For most of us (including myself when God first impressed upon me to fast for forty days), an extended fast seems unattainable, so impossible to do. But we can step out in faith (even with doubts) and say: 'Lord, if this is what you want me to do, with Your help, I'll begin. I'll take it day by day and humble myself before You to listen to You. I desire You, Lord, above all else* (BRIGHT 1997, 25).

I remembered reading Matthew's account of Jesus fasting in the wilderness for forty days. Researching the number forty in the Bible revealed other major historical events. The nation of Israel wandered in the wilderness for forty years. Moses was on Mount Sinai for forty days, and Jesus' disciples saw Him for forty days after His resurrection. Forty days or forty years. These are significant commitments of time. I began praying to God for confirmation on starting a forty-day fast on January 1.

Being a cardiac nurse, Debbie was rightly concerned from a health perspective. I consulted one of my business partners at the time, Dr. Phyllis Gerber, an occupational physician. She mentioned people have medical reasons for extended fasts. Being in good health, I focused on the spiritual benefits rather than health concerns. However, in preparation for this chapter, a little research was needed. In a recent *Healthline* article, "8 Health Benefits of Fasting, Backed by Science," author Rachael Link, MS, RD, wrote, "Despite its recent surge in popularity, fasting is a practice that dates back centuries and plays a central role in many cultures and religions" (Link 2018).

Fasting often involves eliminating food or drinks for a defined period. Regardless of the form of fasting you choose, the goal of biblical fasting is communication with God. As we focus our minds on Him, we experience His presence and provision.

In Matthew, Jesus talked about fasting:

*When you fast, do not look sullen like the hypocrites, for they make their faces unattractive so that people will see them fasting. I tell you the truth, they have their reward! When you fast, anoint your head and wash your face, so that it will not be obvious to others when you are fasting, but only to your Father who is in secret. And your Father, who sees in secret, will reward you* (MATTHEW 6:16-18, NET).

Rereading this passage, I noticed something I had not focused on previously. Twice, Jesus said *when* you. He didn't say *if* you. Instead, he seemed to be emphasizing fasting. *Fasting must be an essential part of growing in relationship with Him.*

### A PENDANT BRINGS PEACE AND HOPE

Over the next several weeks, I continued to pray. On Sunday, December 23, 2007, I went for my walk with Reese and talked to God. We had just passed through an underground tunnel on the return trip heading home. At that moment, I made my decision. Following the guidance in Bill Bright's book, I would do a forty-day fast. I remember it so clearly. I said to God, "I want to grow in my relationship with you, to go deeper. God, I am dedicating this fast to Jennifer. I want information that will help us find her." As soon as those words passed through my mind, I saw light reflecting off the asphalt path. I looked down. Something was lying at the edge of the trail along the grass line. I bent down for a closer look. It was a heart-shaped pendant. As I picked it up and turned it over, it had the name Jennifer inscribed. *What? No way!*

 I froze for a moment. My heart was racing. Where did this pendant come from? I had already passed this spot earlier and didn't see it. What did this mean? After a deep breath, I looked up and said, "Lord, thank you! Thank you for giving me hope. If you have Jennifer's heart, she is in a good place."

*Only by walking with God can we hope to find the path that leads to life. That is what it means to be a disciple. After all—aren't 'we followers of Christ'? Then by all means, let's actually follow him. Not ideas about him. Not just his principles. Him.*
—JOHN ELDREDGE (ELDREDGE 2009, 249)

What a morning! God showed up, offering a silver heart pendant as a tangible expression of His love. He knew my heart was crying out for hope, something I could grasp. I experienced peace, and it felt like a wave had washed over me. At the time, I recalled thinking, *Lord, I don't know if she is with you or waiting to be found. But if you have her heart, that gives me hope.*

My walking pace picked up. I couldn't wait to get home and share this experience with Debbie and the kids. Immediately, I took a picture of that pendant, which has been my mobile phone screen saver since that day. I called Joyce and Drew and shared the photo with them. I knew they needed a tangible expression of hope. The next time we got together, I gave Joyce the pendant.

## MY FIRST FORTY-DAY FAST

Still on an emotional high from my Sunday gift from God, I began my forty-day fast. It was undoubtedly one of the most amazing forty days I had ever experienced. I felt enriched—emotionally, spiritually, and physically.

God showed up and showed off. Amazingly, while subsisting on water and clear broth for forty days, I was not hungry. Bill Bright was right. Committing to knowing the Lord better through fasting provided Him with the opportunity to curb my appetite. By inviting God into my life, I learned nothing is impossible for Him to accomplish. It's for this reason He said *when* you. Eating is a natural and needed source of energy and strength. Through fasting, God wants to demonstrate He can provide that energy and strength without food.

> *Darkness comes. In the middle of it, the future looks blank. The temptation to quit is huge. Don't. You are in good company... You will argue with yourself that there is no way forward. But with God, nothing is impossible. He has more ropes and ladders and tunnels out of pits than you can conceive. Wait. Pray without ceasing. Hope.*
> —JOHN PIPER (PIPER AND KWON 2012)

Fifteen years later, I start each year with a fast. The first ten years were forty-day fasts. However, after donating a kidney in late 2016, I limited the fasting period to twenty-one days.

My prayers for Jenn continue. Our family has no idea when answers will come. However, our hope endures, though the edges are frayed. And I know nothing is impossible for God.

# CHAPTER 11

# DURING WAR

*It's easy to have faith when everything is going great.*
*The real test of faith is when you're facing something*
*that only your faith in God will get you through.*

—GEOFFREY CANADA

*Lord, I ask you to watch over and protect Nick while he is in combat.*
*Bring him and our troops back safely.*

My son, Nicholas, deployed to Iraq in April 2009. He served
in the United States Army as a communications specialist with
the Thirteenth Cavalry Regiment (First Armored Division)
based in Fort Bliss, Texas.

## WHAT WOULD YOU DO?

Nick would have to lean on his faith for the courage to endure
experiences most of us cannot even imagine. I certainly
couldn't. I enlisted in the United States Naval Reserve in July
1975, just as our country's involvement in Vietnam was winding
down. So, I never served in combat. But Nick's grandfather,
Tom Scriffignano, experienced firsthand the importance of
faith to muster courage in war. And he enjoyed sharing his war
stories with Nick. Tom served in the Army's 101st Airborne

division. His glider infantry unit took part in the invasion at Normandy in 1944.

Doing the right thing is challenging under the best conditions. But battlefield conditions and the reality of death is the ultimate test of what and in whom we believe. I began thinking, *What kind of faith do I really have?*

I'm living in the United States. Certainly, many people have endured severe hardships here, just not the ravages of war in many other countries. And we certainly *haven't* faced religious or faith-based persecution as we hear about in other parts of the world. But honestly, my faith and my beliefs have never been tested. I don't know how I would respond. I think I would do the right thing, but would I?

Have you ever watched the TV show, *What Would You Do?* The host, John Quiñones, sets up challenging situations for unsuspecting people to do the right thing. Then, with the use of hidden cameras and audio, the host and the viewing TV audience observe ordinary people responding to these situations. Do they intervene or just sit by and watch? What would you do?

Every episode allows the audience to be the "fly on the wall" and watch how people respond when their beliefs or sense of right or wrong are tested. This is not a hypothetical discussion about what we would do. These individuals are experiencing the raw emotional tension of a "real" situation. What do they do? Will they decide to step up and do something or sit by and do nothing?

In an interview article titled "What Would You Do? Host/ Reporter John Quiñones to Speak at DeVos Place," written by Todd Chance, John shared his thoughts on this show's impact on audiences. Among them, people are put in uncomfortable and awkward situations where they have a choice to make.

Will they move out of their comfort zone and "stand up and do the right thing?" John shared that "most of us are inclined to step away, be safe, and call 911, but there are always heroes who step in—usually it's women." John said something compelling that highlights the "realities" presented in those weekly episodes: "Some schools are even using video clips of the show in sociology and ethics classes" (Chance 2013).

As this is being written, Russia has invaded Ukraine. The world watches with horror the devastating toll war is wreaking on men, women, and children. In addition, globally, historical bias and stereotypes are unveiled as we witness the tensions arising due to religious, cultural, and ethnic prejudices.

History often repeats itself. Alexander Mikutin faced a life-or-death choice. What would he do?

## HOPE INSPIRES COURAGE

 Alexander Mikutin, who was born in the Soviet Union, is the father of my friend and brother in Christ, Anatoly. We met while serving as leaders in the Richmond, Virginia, BSF men's class. During one of our meetings, Anatoly shared with heartfelt passion his father's faith journey in the former Soviet Union.

Alexander Mikutin served as a soldier during World War II around Stalingrad. In December 1941, while walking through the fields of a large collective. He was drawn to a small cabin in the distance where he could see a faint light coming from inside. Standing at the front door, he knocked. An older man invited him to come in from the cold night and get warm. Alexander was amazed at the calm and peaceful demeanor of this older man living in such a sparsely furnished cabin with only a single candle providing light. Alexander noticed a bare shelf that had one book on it and asked, "What's the book about?"

The man didn't answer him. Instead, he walked over to the shelf, picked up the book, and gave it to Alexander. As Alexander's eyes adjusted to the lighting in the room, he realized it was the Bible. Before he could say anything, the man said, "Please take this and read it. But even if you don't read it, hold on to it tightly, and your life will be saved during the war."

Alexander was perplexed and intrigued by the cryptic message and gift. Something stirred within him. He sensed the book was something he needed to read, so he did.

Upon returning to his unit, Alexander began enthusiastically sharing what he was reading with his fellow soldiers. However, many of those soldiers expressed fear and concern for themselves and Alexander. They told him to stop talking about *that* book. The fear was so real they wouldn't even say the word "Bible." They warned him that he would be sent to the frontlines if he kept talking about *that* book.

Reading those soldiers' words in 2023, I wonder, *Why were these men, soldiers, so fearful about reading a Bible or talking about God?*

More than one hundred years ago, communism was introduced into Russia by Vladimir Lenin, the founder of the Russian Communist Party, also known as the Bolsheviks. Lenin inspired and led the Bolshevik Revolution in 1917 and became the first leader of what would become the Union of Soviet Socialist Republics (USSR).

Lenin was enamored with Karl Marx, a German political philosopher famous for advocating communism. Marx coauthored the *Communist Manifesto* with Friedrich Engels. Marx said, "Communism begins where atheism begins" (Frost 2021).

Lenin and Marx envisioned a world and societies without religion of any kind.

As a political science major in college who studied this period of history, Alexander's story immediately captivated me. His story was so compelling, unique, and miraculous because it happened during the tenure of Joseph Stalin, who followed Lenin as the leader of the USSR. In her *History* article "Why Stalin Tried to Stamp Out Religion in the Soviet Union," Natasha Frost wrote:

> *Joseph Stalin, as the second leader of the Soviet Union, tried to enforce militant atheism on the republic. The new "socialist man," Stalin argued, was an atheist one, free of the religious chains that had helped to bind him to class oppression. From 1928 until World War II, when some restrictions were relaxed, the totalitarian dictator shuttered churches, synagogues and mosques and ordered the killing and imprisonment of thousands of religious leaders in an effort to eliminate even the concept of God* (FROST 2021).

With that background, consider Alexander's confidence and belief in what he was reading. He placed his trust and faith in God and the words he read.

Alexander would not keep quiet. Despite the risks, he continued to share boldly. Three days later, he was sent to the frontlines and assigned to be a truck driver. On one mission, as Alexander and six other soldiers traveled down a road, a German plane dropped a bomb on the road near them. The explosion sent the truck tumbling over. All his fellow soldiers were immediately killed. Amazingly, Alexander survived with no injuries.

Recalling that mission, Alexander credited the Bible he kept in the breast pocket of his coat with protecting him from the percussion and shrapnel. From that day on, Alexander's faith strengthened with the older man's words replaying in his mind. When the war ended, Alexander returned home. There, he faithfully read his Bible. The hope he now had encouraged him to share Jesus with family, friends, and neighbors openly.

Then, one day, the KGB unexpectedly showed up at his home and arrested him.

Alexander was brought before the local judge and given a choice. Renounce his belief in God, in Jesus Christ, and stop reading and sharing anything from the Bible, and he would be set free. If not, the judge threatened him with execution or a twenty-five-year sentence to a Gulag. The judge gave him until the following day to make his decision.

I wanted to understand, emotionally, the weight of the decision Alexander was about to make. What was playing out in his heart and mind? I did some research.

Gulags were initially set up by Lenin as forced labor camps. But under Joseph Stalin, Gulags were weaponized against political enemies.

According to the *History* article "Gulag," Gulags were more like forced labor camps. From 1920 to 1953, nearly eighteen million people lived out their sentences in Gulags. The conditions were unspeakable. The article reported, "Prisoners could be required to work up to 14 hours a day, often in extreme weather. Many died of starvation, disease or exhaustion—others were simply executed" (History.com Editors 2018).

In an article, "Letters Depicting the Horrors Lived by Prisoners inside Soviet, Gulags: Gulag, a Word with Thousands of Horrors behind It," Andrei Tapalaga included a story on Arsenii

Formakov (1900–1983), a Latvian poet and journalist convicted of expressing anti-Soviet sentiments in 1940 and sent to a Siberian Gulag for eight years. Formakov wrote about his time in the Gulag. In addition, Emily Johnson, an associate professor at the University of Oklahoma, discovered a weather-worn letter among documents in 2011. The following paragraph is from an article by Emily from one of Formakov's letters:

> *Now that everything is in the past, I can say that four months last year (from August until I was injured) were physically very difficult for me. Sometimes you pull yourself up to the car with a cross on your shoulder, one that is heavy, damp and has the texture of a log. You're sweaty, your heartbeat is so strong that you feel like it's going to jump out of your chest, you're breathing so hard that you start panting like a horse and you start thinking: let your foot give way. You will fall and cross, it will fall on you and this will be the end: there will be no more suffering and everything will end forever!*
> (TAPALAGA AND JOHNSON 2022)

I remember thinking Alexander had to know about the atrocities and conditions of the Gulags, which makes his story more compelling.

That night, Alexander prayed fervently. Finally, he knew what he needed to do. Around 4 a.m., Alexander described a sense of calm and peace. He felt God's presence with him and clearly heard he would only be in prison for three years. Several hours later, before the judge, Alexander said, "I am not a criminal, and I've done nothing wrong. But for the sake of God, I will accept fifty years in prison."

In disbelief, the judge said, "Young man, you will regret your decision," and sentenced him to a Gulag in Siberia.

Alexander arrived in a Gulag that housed murderers and prisoners who had committed other serious offenses. They asked him why he ended up in this Gulag. Alexander told them he had been sentenced for reading the Bible and talking about God. The other prisoners couldn't believe it. He boldly shared his war experiences and the hope he found in Jesus. As a result, many of his fellow prisoners accepted Jesus as their Savior and Lord.

Ironically, Alexander's influence had a calming effect on the Gulag. The overall atmosphere improved day by day. These men were becoming nicer to each other and to the guards.

The Gulag authorities noticed the changes and, rather than celebrate the reduced tension, transferred Alexander to another facility. Immediately after arriving in his new "home," he continued sharing his faith and good news with his fellow prisoners. When they observed his confidence and courage, many invited Jesus into their lives. His positive impact on the Gulag was rewarded with another transfer. Alexander embraced the change as another opportunity to share Christ with a new group of prisoners.

Finally, the authorities had enough of Alexander. They decided he was more "dangerous" in prison and decided to set him free. The day of his release was precisely three years from the day he was sentenced to the first Gulag in Siberia.

Returning home would not be easy. Anatoly remembered the KGB assigned three or four men who followed his every step. Occasionally, they would come to his home and search to ensure his father wasn't hiding religious material or Bibles. Nevertheless, Alexander continued sharing Christ with his community. He collected Bibles and hymn books so the community could read and worship. In addition, Alexander handwrote content to be shared.

Knowing the KGB would confiscate any religious material, he built birdhouses to hide them. Eventually, twenty good-sized birdhouses were on his property. Alexander reasoned the KGB would never think to look inside them. Instead, they thought he was peculiar and called him the bird man. The community's hiding place remained a secret.

Alexander's enthusiasm and courage inspired his neighbors to live out their faith boldly. As a result, the community experienced peace, despite the difficult times. But there was a cost.

Alexander was fined by the authorities several times. Yet, as a seven-year-old, Anatoly said, "My family and neighbors were a wonderful community. Everyone helped each other during challenging times."

Soviet authorities did not allow people to gather for religious purposes openly. So, people met in each other's homes and the forest, even in the coldest months. Anatoly said it was unbelievable to see people gather outside in the cold to worship together. He specifically remembered how excited people were after they had accepted Jesus into their lives. When someone wanted to be baptized immediately, they went to the closest water, a lake or river. They even cut a hole in the ice so people could be baptized.

Anatoly vividly remembers the enthusiasm and excitement of those people who wanted to be baptized in December in Russia. He witnessed extraordinary boldness and courage in his community. He told me, "The darker the days and nights were, the brighter the hope, as we united as one family, God's family."

During our interview, Anatoly said he felt privileged to have a father so committed to sharing his faith, despite the real risks. His father lived out what he believed and loved everyone unconditionally.

Anatoly smiled and shared his father had one house rule. He and his sibling were required to read one or two chapters in the Bible every day before they could eat breakfast. He laughed, saying, "No one wanted to miss breakfast, so we read from the Bible every morning."

## THE KGB PLANS TO BREAK UP ANATOLY'S FAMILY

As Anatoly continued sharing his experiences growing up, he got emotional. The KGB knew his father continued practicing his faith. They hatched a plan to break up the family. They would send his siblings to different schools. Unfortunately, some of the schools were a great distance from home.

The KGB expected to break his father's will by breaking his children's will. They believed the children were the weak link. The plan backfired as they quickly realized the parent's faith, confidence, and courageousness passed onto the kids. As a family, they endured severe testing together.

Anatoly described the bullying he suffered from other students, encouraged by teachers. He and his siblings were branded as "Christians," stupid, and naive. He was told he would never amount to anything. However, thanks to his parents' example, all his brothers and sisters survived and thrived.

Anatoly graduated from medical school in 1985, married his Ukrainian wife, and had three children. He completed a family medicine residency program in 1988. Anatoly thrived, supported by his family and his faith in God.

He told me about something unexpected that had happened. The KGB agents assigned to his father realized he was no threat, and they became Christians after listening to him, seeing his courage, and how everyone in the community lived.

Anatoly recalled when President Ronald Reagan visited the Brandenburg Gate in West Berlin, Germany, and challenged Mikhail Gorbachev, the leader of the Soviet Union, to end the Cold War by tearing down the wall (Reagan 2021). After that, his family realized significant changes and uncertainty were coming.

In August of 1989, Anatoly had an opportunity to obtain a visa from Israel. This allowed him and his family to leave the country. They planned on living in the United States. However, that same year brought another surprise: his father, now seventy-five, had his record expunged by the former Soviet Union.

I asked Anatoly what kept him connected to his family still in the Soviet Union. He said, "I watched my parents live by faith, trusting God would always provide, because He had many times, over many years. I knew I could trust God during difficult times."

Anatoly finally met the United States' requirements as a new citizen and was able to invite his family to join him. In 1992, his father and other family came to the United States. However, before his father left, he was allowed to experience another miracle.

The local judge who had sentenced Alexander to the Siberian Gulag nearly fifty years earlier tracked him down and arranged to connect with him at the local train station.

When they met, the judge asked Alexander for forgiveness, saying he regretted his actions and explaining he was just carrying out his orders. The judge then asked Alexander if he still had the older man's Bible. Alexander said he did, and they arranged to meet again. He gave that Bible to the judge. A great example of grace, the power of forgiveness, and that nothing is impossible for God.

Alexander's courageous, hope-filled journey from a soldier in World War II, to a prisoner in Soviet Union Gulags, to the "bird man" watched by the KGB for years, to a citizen of the United States of America at the age of ninety-two is truly remarkable. God worked miraculously through Alexander's life. He impacted countless lives, including mine. His ripple effect of courageous faith will continue through the telling of his story in this book.

**REFLECTIONS**

We all believe in something. It is easy to believe something until it is tested. Alexander's story caused me to think seriously about whether I had the confidence and character to believe so strongly that I would be willing to risk my life. Would I do the right thing when tested?

How strongly do you believe what you believe? Would you be willing to sacrifice everything you own, including your life, for what you believe in? What would you do?

Jim Baker, former Secretary of State under President George H. W. Bush, said, "Proper preparation prevents poor performance" (Baker 2020). Therefore, preplanning is an excellent place to start to ensure we *will* always do the right thing.

I attended a virtual conference conducted by Donald Miller on productivity in 2020. In the opening session, Donald referenced Habit 2 from Stephen R. Covey's well-known book *The 7 Habits of Highly Effective People.* Habit 2 is an excellent place to begin planning because it challenges us to "begin with the end in mind." However, in his twist on Habit 2, Donald challenged the participants to write their own obituaries. That puts us in the position to think with the end in mind.

The following were a few of the critical questions we were challenged to answer:

*Is there a big vision you want to accomplish before you pass? If so, what is it? What individuals in your life do you want to show a lifetime of love and devotion to? What do you want people to feel on the day they find out you are gone? List four things that matter most to you about life. What are your core values?* (MILLER 2020, 4)

Consider using this framework, and write your own obituary. What would you want people to say about you?

The bottom line is this: Do you and I want what we wrote in our obituary to be true about us? Do we want to be a positive influence in the lives of others? If the answer is yes, develop the discipline to live purposefully with the end in mind.

> *Discipline is the ability to make yourself do something you don't want to do in order to get a result you really want to get.*
>
> —ANDY ANDREWS (ANDREWS 2020)

# CHAPTER 12

# AFTER IDENTITY CRISIS

*Men are being told LIES about what it means to be a man – and it's literally killing us. We're exhausted from the constant pressure, loneliness and feeling like we never measure up.*

—ROBERT LEWIS

I am grateful for the people who came alongside me during my quest to become a better man, husband, and father.

While "it takes a community" may be a bit overused, my experience confirms it's true. We were not meant to live life alone. Unfortunately, I often felt my success was all about my effort. I bought into the idea of wanting to be a "self-made" man. Looking back, it's hard to imagine any level of success without support, training, and mentoring. Focusing on *self* has a way of clouding reality. The truth is we all have benefited from the investments of many people. No one is self-made.

In a *BBC Worklife* article titled "Why We Define Ourselves by Our Jobs," author Kate Morgan said, "We often see our jobs as a defining detail of who we are, yet too closely tying our identities to work can be dangerous. What can we do about it?" (Morgan 2021).

The topic of work comes up naturally, almost instinctively, in conversations. I recall thinking how important it was to define myself by my work, my title, and what I was doing.

One factor contributing to seeking identity in our work is a three-letter word: ego. Our ego can be helpful when harnessed correctly, or it will harm us when left unchallenged. In her article "The Two Sides of Your Ego and How to Balance Them," Skylar Rae summarized information she learned from a Jay Shetty podcast about overcoming the ego. Skylar focused on how to find the proper balance.

The harmful ego is self-focused, causing us to put the negative things in our lives into an audio soundtrack that repeats, "Why am I such a loser? I just look so terrible today, I don't feel like doing anything, or everything is going completely wrong" (Rae 2021). The result is an energy drain that discourages people and creates despair.

The helpful ego's focus is on being acutely aware of our actions, attitudes, words, and emotions in a way that encourages, motivates, and energizes us to push forward daily. Skylar offered the following comment:

The most amazing and interesting thing about these two sides is that the ego is truly responsible for each! The struggle in this is being able to balance both the harmful and healthy self-focus in a way that creates a *balanced ego*. The balance point of the ego is humility. Humility is the ability to be aware of your success or importance and use it to uplift you yet also be able to detach from it and become a modest observer (Rae 2021).

We face the challenge of unknowingly combining who we are with what we do. In so doing, it becomes the primary focus of our interactions with people. Finding identity in our work limits opportunities to get to know people—their backgrounds, families, and outside work interests. When our lives are wrapped around work, it's going to impact "listening" to the people in our lives and learning about their hopes, aspirations, hobbies, hang-ups, and passions.

Unfortunately, when our lives are out of focus, the people and relationships that matter most suffer. This was certainly my story, and I'm not alone. Sadly, a heavy focus on work defining our identities and self-worth often leads to not "seeing" people and ourselves correctly. We become blind to reality.

The predictable result was articulated well by Anne Wilson in the *BBC Worklife* article:

> *If you tie [your self-worth] to your career, the successes and failures you experience will directly affect your self-worth* (MORGAN 2021).

A potential side effect of finding identity in our work is a condition I'm calling *egorelattionalmyopia* (ego-relational-myopia). If this were an actual medical ailment, its description might read:

> *A condition typically found in people who suffer from being self-focused. It is characterized by a strong ego. It is difficult to diagnose due to the patient's inability to see and interpret the warning signs. If left untreated, it will harm relationships.*

Sounds serious. I had a form of this condition many years ago. It almost destroyed my marriage. I was diagnosed shortly after Jenn's abduction. Unfortunately, many people live with this condition, undiagnosed.

## BLINDSIDED

Alex and I met in 1971 while playing on the high school tennis team. Alex was good, but I was not. As a teenager, it was more important to be *on* the team. We both got married in 1980—Alex and Nellie in June, Debbie and I in November. It's hard to believe over fifty years have passed. We remained friends while raising families, climbing our respective careers ladders, and navigating through everyday life.

Alex's career path included quite a bit of travel and multiple relocations. Like any good friendship, whenever we got together, we picked up where we left off. Our conversations often centered around our jobs and families. Alex was in senior management for several large companies. I was always impressed with his professionalism and expertise. I sought his counsel repeatedly over the years.

Whenever we talked, the conversations primarily focused on work-related topics. We also talked about the various places we traveled to on business. Alex had the opportunity to travel internationally. I always found his observations and insights on the similarities and differences in business in other countries informative.

One aspect of our conversations always caught my attention and raised the hair on the back of my neck. It was about dinner meetings. You're thinking, *Dinner meetings? What's the big deal?* Well, normally nothing, except when you share too many details with your wife—who is home alone with the kids. It's not likely to go over well. And it didn't.

We both have great wives: loving, caring, nurturing, and patient. We both had young children, and our wives worked while raising our kids. The truth was that Debbie and Nellie carried the lion's share of the responsibility in our respective homes. This included taking care of the physical home, the kids, school, baths, sports-related activities, cooking, cleaning, disciplining, and doctor's appointments. Did I miss anything? I think you're beginning to see the picture. Without realizing it, when Alex shared about his business trips with Nellie and talked about the expensive restaurants he had visited, it was more details than needed.

After Alex shared with me one day, his tone shifted to disappointment as he said, "When I'm talking to Nellie about my day, she gets mad at me."

I traveled quite a bit for business as well and ate in expensive restaurants. That's not the problem. I had been sharing too many details with Debbie too, and it didn't go well. Nothing is worse than being away from home and having a stressful discussion with your spouse. With those conversations burned into my mind, I kept my calls brief. On any given night, Debbie and the kids were eating hot dogs, mac and cheese, pizza, or whatever. They were *not* eating expensive meals at fancy restaurants. And our wives were *not* getting dressed up to go out and have adult conversations *without* kids.

Alex and I shared a similar challenge. We couldn't *see* or connect the context I just described—*before* talking with our wives. Overcoming this challenge required putting ourselves in our wives' shoes and appreciating the sacrifices *they* were making while we were traveling on business. I was not surprised by Nellie's response.

In one of our conversations, I shared with Alex how I chose to share my day with Debbie. My report of the day's activities was matter-of-fact. "You know, boring meetings, okay hotels, a quick bite to eat, catch up on work emails, and go to bed."

Don't hear this the wrong way. I'm not saying I lied. I'm saying I chose to consider what Debbie's situation was *first* and wisely avoided sharing too much information. I just didn't want to start an argument. Using the analogy of "what happens in Vegas, stays in Vegas" may be overkill. You get my point. We don't benefit from sharing more details than needed. Period.

When our focus is on what *we're* doing, it's going to prevent us from seeing what is right in front of us. Add our egos, and you have a powder keg ready to be lit. Seeking identity in our work is exhausting. No wonder we don't have time for anyone else.

*Pastor Tim Keller said, "If our identity is in our work, rather than Christ, success will go to our heads, and failure will go to our hearts"* (KELLER 2015).

Ouch!

## REALITY CHECK

On Easter Sunday, April 4, 2010, I received a call from Alex at 8 a.m. I recall thinking it was odd he would call so early on a holiday. When I answered the call, he was emotional. His words conveyed concern and fear. He simply asked if I would be home and available to talk with him later. He was on his way home from dropping Nellie off at the airport.

No one enjoys cryptic phone calls. It leaves us wondering what the heck is going on. I immediately thought something had happened to his mother. During our high school years, I spent a lot of time at Alex's home and was close to his mother.

When Alex called back, he was agitated and struggled to speak. The pause was palpable. Now I was really concerned. Finally, he said, "On the way to the airport, Nellie told me she had met with an attorney and wanted a divorce."

*What?* If we had been in person, the looks on our faces would have told some story. My heart sank. His words sounded eerily familiar. Debbie and I were in that place in 2005, before Jennifer's abduction.

Alex told me he was taken completely by surprise. He had no clue anything was wrong with their marriage. His words and voice revealed he was searching for answers, trying to understand what had happened.

As we talked over the course of the day, our conversations felt more like counseling sessions. In between phone calls, I thanked God for working with me over the past four years and prompting Alex to call me, just as He prompted me to call Bill Rush back on April 10, 2006. At that time, Bill offered the hope I needed. Now I was honored to offer hope and encouragement to Alex.

In every conversation, we dug a little deeper. I asked questions based on what Alex was sharing. I could feel the pain he felt. He was on an emotional rollercoaster. We finally dug deep enough. The snapshot picture of their marriage relationship was getting clearer to me.

Nellie did not *want* a divorce. She wanted Alex's *attention.* She wanted to be heard. I had no doubt in my mind Alex may have *heard* the words Nellie spoke. He wasn't actively *listening.*

After prayer and reflection, I finally felt comfortable sharing my thoughts. With a calm, confident voice, I said, "Alex, I have one question: Have you been listening to what you have been telling me today?"

Alex, in a low voice, said, "Yes."

"Good," I replied, "because what I've gathered from what you shared is Nellie has been trying to get your attention. She's been crying out for help. She wants to have meaningful conversations with you." Over the phone, I sensed he was squirming a little, trying to figure out where I was going in this conversation. I said clearly and bluntly, "Nellie doesn't want a divorce."

Alex pushed back loudly, "Didn't you hear what I told you earlier? Nellie made it clear in the car that she wants a divorce!"

I pushed back as forcefully by repeating specific conversations, saying, "From what you told me, Nellie has tried to get your attention several times, but you weren't picking up her cues. In her mind, she had no choice but to talk to an attorney. I believe it was to get your attention."

We had a brief pause in the conversation. "Does she have your attention now?" I asked.

After another quiet pause, Alex said, "Yes."

"Good. Let's talk about what needs to happen next," I offered.

I had traveled a path similar to Alex's. Based on my recent experience, I was able to share some suggestions to help open a conversation with Nellie when she got back home.

First, I firmly suggested to Alex, "You need to own this entire situation, do not get into the blame game, and don't expect Nellie to own any responsibility."

Alex interrupted me. "Marriage is a two-way street. Both of us have a responsibility in this." His voice revealed how deeply he was hurting.

I allowed a pause in the conversation, then said, "Alex, what you're saying is true, but in this instance, it's too late. Is your approach going to help the situation? Both of you are hurt right now. I want you to take the lead."

While attending our church in Orlando, Dr. David Uth preached a sermon on marriage. He offered a visual illustration I've never forgotten. Cupping his two hands together, he described marriage as two warped boards that come together. Over time, the two boards are slowly drawn together through the pressures and stresses of life, becoming solidly connected. Dr. Uth shared we often focus on trying to change our spouses. We expect quick results and lose patience. To illustrate his point, he cupped his hands again, this time quickly snapping them together. I still hear that sound. And after a pause, he said relationships break when we don't allow the pressures of life, stress, and time to work on drawing couples together in a sustainable way. Debbie and I looked at each other, heads nodding in agreement. This would have been helpful to know early in our marriage.

I reminded Alex of my journey. Jenn's abduction was my clarifying moment, bringing me to my knees. He was having his moment, so own it. Besides, neither of us had been conducting ourselves in a God-honoring way as husbands and fathers. How could we have? We didn't know God, so we had no idea of His expectations or how to pursue healthy relationships with our wives and kids.

By about 9 p.m. that night, our conversations were calmer and more productive. With a reassuring voice, I explained to Alex, "It's okay if you don't agree with everything Nellie has said to you, but you do need to respect her perspective. It's how she's processing years of frustration and how she is seeing your relationship." I encouraged him by letting him know this was the path I took with Debbie. It relieved the anxiety and stress at the time.

**DECISION TIME**

"Alex, we talked off and on all day today. I know it's been stressful, but I hope it's been helpful. You won't be able to rebuild your relationship with Nellie without God's help." I paused. "Do you want God's help?

Without hesitation, Alex replied, "Yes!"

We prayed together, and Alex, with confidence and certainty in his voice that had been missing all day, surrendered his life to Christ. He told me he wanted to become a better husband and father to make his marriage work.

We then discussed his next steps. Mimicking Bill Rush's question from back in April 2006, I asked Alex whether he had a Bible. I recommended the *Every Man's Bible*, the one I had bought. He began reading and studying, and we started sharing life together in a new way.

Before we ended our conversation that night, I wanted to ensure that Alex understood some challenges and setbacks were ahead. It's part of acknowledging our past while growing and maturing.

Knowing Alex as well as I did, I offered a warning. It would be his sole responsibility to always exhibit self-control and restraint in every conversation with Nellie and his kids. He would need to be patient like never before. I shared that based on my experience, don't expect your family to embrace your words; they'll need to see consistent actions. "You didn't get into this situation overnight, and you're not getting out overnight; it's going to take time."

The bottom line: actions and attitude would speak louder than anything he would say. I added, "Please do not talk about your decision tonight as if it will miraculously fix years of dysfunction. It won't."

The last thing I recommended was that he start praying for Nellie and his kids. Only God can work in their hearts. Let Him work in them, just like He will work in you.

## REFLECTIONS

From that day on, Alex invested in becoming a better man, husband, father, and friend. He wanted his family to have the best version of himself. Fortunately for Alex, Nellie's strong faith gave her strength and patience all those years and would sustain them now. She was in his corner, by his side, praying for him daily.

Alex became an avid reader of the Bible while also reading and listening to various inspiring and encouraging content. He joined a BSF men's class and studied the Gospel of John. To this day, Alex remains committed to a preferred future and cooperates with the Holy Spirit to live his new life.

Over the years since that Easter 2010 conversation, we have gotten together as couples several times. We all agree and acknowledge that without God's intervention, without each other for support, we all would be in very different places.

Thankfully, each of us worked at restoring our relationships by offering forgiveness and encouraging each other. I told Alex many times that I was so proud to see him immediately and aggressively embrace the brutal facts of his life and the transformation only God can do.

It has been an honor to walk with Alex and Nellie. It is an incredible blessing to witness the miracles of God rescuing us from our messes, redeeming the damage, and restoring us to a right relationship with Himself and with the people in our lives.

## BIG TAKEAWAYS

- Be fully present and engaged in every conversation, especially with your spouse.
- Keep your focus on God, not work or other substitutes.
- Remain connected physically and spiritually with other people. Life is better in community.
- Recognize the early signs that your life is drifting.

# CHAPTER 13

# AFTER DRIFTING

*Direct your children onto the right path, and*
*when they are older, they will not leave it.*

—KING SOLOMON

Many believe acquiring things, achieving social or work status, and financial independence will make them happy. Seeking happiness proves challenging because it's an elusive goal, like trying to grab and hold onto the air we breathe. Why do I say that? Because, generally, we only describe being happy when things in our lives are good.

Life comes with financial and relational stress and, often, family discord. Our calendars reveal lives overwhelmed by commitments and busyness. Most days, we're not happy. Life seems out of control. This was true in my life for many years. Then I realized happiness shouldn't be my primary goal.

Unfortunately, that realization only came after Jennifer's abduction. In quiet moments, I began an intense time of self-reflection to face the honest truths about my life. You may have experienced some catalytic event in your life and understand the aftermath.

Maintaining appearances and "keeping up with the Joneses" is exhausting. Why are we so concerned about what other people think about us? Sadly, I focused more on what other people thought of me at the expense of my wife and kids. Is this what life is supposed to be? Intuitively, I knew the answer was no. There had to be some meaning and purpose for my life. But what? I would soon learn *in* whom my priority must be.

I faced an important truth: my life had been drifting because it wasn't anchored to a specific plan and to *the* right person. In hindsight, it's clear we don't drift toward something; it's usually toward nothing or nowhere. And worse, drifting operates in stealth mode. It doesn't draw attention to itself. It just happens. And then, one day, *bam*—you're jolted back into reality.

## SCOTT'S JOURNEY

Debbie and I first heard Scott Harrison speak while watching a Northpoint Ministries message series titled "Voices" on July 26, 2017 (Harrison 2017). Scott shared authentically about his life, struggles, and triumphs. We've all heard a picture is worth a thousand words, and the photos and messaging Scott shared that morning were powerful.

Scott was born in Philadelphia to an average middle-class family. His father was an engineer and businessman, and his mother was a writer and journalist. In 1979 when he was four years old, his family moved to a house in the suburbs. It didn't have good curb appeal, but it reduced his father's work commute.

Scott got emotional as he recounted that inside their home was an unknown and unseen problem that would change his family's life. Soon after moving in, his mother got busy fixing the basement. Then, one New Year's Day, as she walked across her bedroom, she collapsed, unconscious on the floor. They took her to the local hospital and ran some tests, including blood samples.

When they got the results, it was not good. His mother had been exposed to a colorless, odorless gas called carbon monoxide that prevented the proper transport of oxygen throughout her body.

Scott's family learned the local gas company had improperly installed the furnace. Remember, this was 1979, and the first carbon monoxide detectors weren't available until 1993. It wasn't until years later that they were required in homes with gas, oil, or coal-burning appliances.

Thankfully, Scott's mother recovered, but she was never the same. Her immune system had been compromised. She went from being a healthy super mom to being weak and sickly, seemingly overnight. Her immune system reacted to almost any chemical, including perfumes, cologne, car fumes, and the ink used in book printing. And that was a problem for his journalist mother.

As I write this, the world has been under various masking and other personal protective requirements for nearly two years to reduce the spread of the COVID-19 virus. We all know how challenging and cumbersome this was for even brief periods. Pause for a minute and roll back to 1979. Scott's mother had to wear a charcoal mask and gloves all the time. She had to put books in a plastic bag so she could read them.

His parents had a solid Christian faith. Despite the seriousness of the situation, they chose not to sue the gas company for their negligence. His father decided to find and repair the gas leak. Scott's parents firmly believed God would provide for their needs. And, importantly, they did not want to live bitter or resentful.

My family and I would have benefited from that kind of faith. In 1992, while working in banking, a physician client offered me an opportunity to get in on a real estate deal. He and his partners wanted to buy lots at a municipal tax sale. As a thirty-something-year-old with three kids at the time, the commission being offered would have been very helpful.

When I shared my exciting opportunity with Debbie, an RN in a local hospital, she warned, "Don't get involved with that group of doctors." She was aware of them, and they were not to be trusted. She asked if I had the agreement in writing. I said no. After all, these were doctors, one of whom was a client I knew. I believed his handshake was enough. Wrong.

After the sale, this client and his partners didn't pay me the commission we had agreed to. I was crazy angry and wanted to sue them. I talked to an attorney who quickly pointed out that verbal agreements can be enforced and taken to court, *except* when it involves real estate.

This situation is not even close to what the Harrisons faced. The lesson learned—regardless of the circumstances—was we are always in control of our response. Scott's parents chose to focus on God to provide. They opted for peace over bitterness. I depended on myself and my wisdom. I chose to seek a legal remedy and became angry, bitter, and resentful.

### IN ONE MOMENT, EVERYTHING CHANGED

Scott grew up as an only child and took on a caregiver role for his mom. He helped around the house, including cooking. He learned to play the piano and soon found himself in the worship band at his church. Scott described himself as a good Christian kid and avoided smoking, swearing, drinking alcohol, or experimenting with drugs. He was a rule follower.

At age eighteen, he had enough of playing by the rules. It was exhausting, and he wanted to be doing what his friends were doing. He grew his hair to shoulder length, joined a band, and moved to New York City. Fame and fortune in rock and roll called. Unfortunately, that ride lasted one month as the band members realized they hated each other.

Scott decided to stay in New York City. It was the 1980s, and he quickly learned people have plenty of opportunities if they sought rebellion. He accepted an offer to be a nightclub promoter, an excellent job for a rebel—get paid to drink alcohol for free. All he had to do was encourage people to come to the nightclub.

He recalled the extravagance of people paying twenty dollars for a cocktail and five hundred for a bottle of champagne. Over the next ten years, he would climb the social nightlife ladder in New York City.

It's incredible how, when we are young, we're so focused on being successful without necessarily having a clear goal. Our egos take control of our minds. Right after Debbie and I married, I worked for my dad's business at age twenty-four. Quickly, I went from a sales rep to regional sales manager to, finally, national sales manager. I remember proudly wearing my three-piece suit to meetings and handing out cards with "National Sales Manager" on them. You can't pay the rent or buy food with your ego. Only with hindsight and maturity do we recognize the foolishness of seeking to satisfy our ego. I know I'm not alone.

When we're so impressed with ourselves, we do the craziest things. Scott recalled intentionally exposing his wrist so some photographer he didn't know would take a picture of him wearing a Rolex watch.

He was living the dream, or so he thought. Dinners at 10 p.m. The club scene after midnight. An after-hours party at 5 a.m. Bed at noon. During the ten years of this life, Scott took advantage of every vice that came his way—marijuana, ecstasy, and cocaine. He smoked two packs of cigarettes daily and had a gambling problem. He was into pornography and strip clubs.

The pursuit of happiness is an elusive goal. We try to fill the voids in our hearts with the forbidden, only to realize those fleeting, feel-good moments never satisfy or provide happiness. While Scott shared his go-to vices, I shook my head in agreement.

For me, alcohol served two purposes: it was socially acceptable, and it offered relief from life's stresses. It deadened the senses enough to forget about them briefly. Viewing pornographic images was an easy fix to experience those desirable "feelings." One of the downsides to the internet is that inappropriate and unhelpful content just pops up. What was once viewed as pornography is now accepted as part of many advertisements. Those images catch our eyes and attention, and off we go, drifting.

Scott began to wrestle with himself. *How did I get into this life?* He had drifted so far away from the example of his Christian parents. Thankfully, his childhood memories and parents helped him find his way back.

## TIPPING POINT

Scott traveled with friends to a big party town in South America. They rented a house with servants and horses and bought one thousand dollars worth of fireworks to go along with magnums of Dom Perignon. In his sober moments, he told himself, *I'm living the good life. I have a grand piano, BMW,*

*Rolex watch, girlfriend, a labrador retriever, and I appeared on the cover of magazines.* On this trip, something began stirring within him. *I've become the worst person I know. Bankrupt morally, emotionally, and spiritually.* Scott realized if he continued this path, the legacy he would leave behind would be absolutely nothing. His tombstone would read, "Here lies a man who's gotten a million people wasted over the course of his life. Bravo."

What was it that King Solomon said? "Direct your children onto the right path, and when they are older, they will not leave it" (Proverbs 22:6, NLT).

Scott's faith-filled and loving parents never gave up on him. They regularly sent encouraging emails to remind him who he was. His father even sent reading material to take on his trip. He began reading something by A.W. Tozer, an American pastor and author. Then he started reading his Bible. He was confronted with brutal facts about his current life.

Returning home, Scott was determined to change his life radically. He wanted to serve others. His transformation journey would take a few months to sort out.

He began by selling everything he owned, including his car and Rolex. Nearly two thousand DVDs went on eBay in one single lot. He gave up the apartment in New York and moved out of the city. Now, he had to find work that was the opposite of his former life. He applied to several well-known humanitarian organizations. He planned to work one year of service for the ten years he selfishly wasted.

Then, reality hit. Every organization turned him down. He said, "They wouldn't touch me with a ten-foot pole." Why? "These organizations were doing important work worldwide while I'm getting a thousand people drunk every night. Not a great resume."

One day an organization offered him the opportunity to join them by going to a country he had never heard of, Liberia. All he had to do was pay them five hundred dollars a month. Smiling, Scott said, "That sounded perfect. It is the opposite of what I was doing and how I was living. Go to a place you never heard of and pay for the opportunity to do so."

The organization was Mercy Ships. Their mission is to offer safe surgeries to people without access. They report that five billion people need various health procedures. Sadly, that number includes children, teens, and adults who suffer and die every day from treatable conditions. Fifty percent of the world's population lives near a coast, and this organization deploys hospital ships to provide the needed medical care. (Mercy Ships Mission).

Within a few months, Scott set to sail for West Africa on a 522-foot Mercy Ship. He was a volunteer photojournalist. His degree in communications from New York University would help. He also had a massive list of contacts from his nightclub days.

As Scott stood on the ship gangway, he knew he had made the right decision to quit his past life. Now, by faith, he stepped into a new story. But to be part of the story God had for him required radical obedience. So, from that day on, he gave up smoking, gambling, strip clubs, and pornography. This may be radical from the world's view, but Scott now had his eyes focused on God.

### REALITY IS HEARTBREAKING

Upon arrival in Monrovia, Scott noticed hundreds of people living in apartment buildings with no glass in the windows. Once-beautiful houses were left wholly destroyed by past wars. Bullet holes were observable everywhere. He started taking pictures of this broken country.

At 5 a.m., on the third day in Liberia, Scott packed his cameras into a Land Rover and, along with staff, traveled to the football stadium that served as a triage location. He wondered whether anyone would show up. As they turned a corner toward the stadium, he saw thousands of people outside the stadium doors.

Scott emotionally responded to what he saw and photographed. So many people with physical disabilities. He shared photos with his email list from years in the nightclub scene. Quickly, the list began to shrink as people hit the unsubscribe button. Previously, these people were on his list to learn about the next party. They weren't interested in seeing pictures of people with medical conditions. However, the photos did move some people, sparking a desire to help by donating money. Some decided to volunteer by serving people in need. Scott learned the images and stories had the power to move people toward personal involvement and being compassionate and giving.

He traveled to rural areas and saw people drinking dirty water for the first time. He was appalled they had no option but to drink contaminated water. Before this experience, water was a ten-dollar bottle of Voss. His nightclubs sold it to people who generally took a few sips and threw the bottle away.

Quite a contrast to the people he observed who had no choice but to drink from ponds and rivers. What he saw was repulsive. He wouldn't let his dog drink that water. Scott met a thirteen-year-old girl who only had access to dirty water her entire life for drinking, cooking, and bathing.

Back on the ship, Scott shared what he saw with the doctors. They told him many diseases worldwide are caused by bad water. This issue struck a nerve with Scott. The doctors suggested this was an issue he should tackle.

*Start by doing what's necessary; then do what's possible; and suddenly you are doing the impossible.*
—FRANCIS OF ASSISI (ASSISI & DOUGHERTY 2021)

Scott went to work on it. At the time, nearly 660 million people worldwide were drinking bad water every day. A staggering number of people, almost a tenth of the world's population. Why? Because of where they happened to be born, not through any choice they made.

Listening to Scott's emotional epiphany, I couldn't imagine having to drink dirty, unsafe water every day. While this seemed unfathomable, it was true and remains so today.

Scott brought back a bottle of that water and had it tested at a lab in New York. The results were shocking. The water contained a variety of live amoebas and parasites. And this is the water people were drinking and bathing in every day.

Scott had a purpose; a passion was ignited. He would bring clean water to vulnerable populations. He believed this issue was solvable and said:

*There's not a single person on earth that needs to drink dirty water right now. It's not like some of these diseases that were looking for cures in test tubes, maybe decades in the future. We know how to give clean water to every human being right now. We don't have the will to do it. We haven't allocated the resources.*

With a clear vision, Scott founded Charity: Water. He shared what he had seen with a message of hope:

*I want to see a day on earth when everyone has*
*clean water regardless of where they were born.*

The challenge was how and where to begin. He learned many people don't trust charities, so they don't give; 42 percent of Americans distrust charities, and 70 percent believe charities waste money. Scott knew if he wanted to make a difference, he would have to do something different. Tackling the seemingly impossible task of bringing clean water to thousands of people would also require reinventing a better charitable organization model. This would be critical if he wanted to encourage thousands of people and companies to give time and money generously.

Scott reimagined how a charity could operate: "First, we had a problem dealing with the money. How much money is going to reach the people needing clean water? What if we created a way where 100 percent of every donation would go straight to the projects and people?"

Almost immediately, he was told it was a dumb idea. How are you going to pay your staff and your overhead? Scott had an idea. First, he opened two bank accounts. One was for public money. One hundred percent of that money would fund projects. Scott was determined to personally raise funds needed to cover overhead costs through people and businesses that shared his vision. The second account would be for that purpose.

Second, Scott wanted to provide evidence that donated money was making a difference. That required building a hyper-transparent organization. Water projects were put on Google Earth and Google Maps so anybody from the public could observe the progress. And third, Charity: Water would work with local partners. Scott believed that for the work to be sustainable, it had to be led by local people in the countries they would serve.

At the time, many people thought this was a crazy idea. But it worked.

Charity: Water was founded in 2006. According to their website, 91,414 water projects have been funded as of this writing, and over 14.7 million people have been served in twenty-nine countries (About us: Charity: Water).

I believe Scott is right. As a world community, we can bring clean water to every person in need. We don't have the will to do it. Inaction speaks louder than words. You and I can make a difference – by supporting organizations like Charity Water.

**REFLECTIONS**

Drifting through life can be hazardous for your health, wealth, and relationships. Drifting occurs when you have no purpose or plan. I believe drifting is in the same category as not making decisions. They go together. We may struggle with making good or the right decisions, but not making decisions is, in fact, a decision!

On January 5, 2014, Pastor Andy Stanley began a sermon series called *Ask It*. Over the next six weeks, Debbie and I watched online. That first Sunday, we learned the importance of questioning every decision that might impact relationships, marriages, finances, and our health. Some of the goals of asking the right questions include reducing complexity and stress, fewer financial issues, and less regret, which would reduce the number of times we have to apologize for something to someone. Debbie and I looked at each other many times wishing we had heard this early in our marriage. What was the question? Here it is:

*In light of your past experience, your current circumstances,*
*and your future hopes and dreams, what is the wise thing*
*for you to do?* (STANLEY 2013)

Wow! I believe this question is so powerful because the focus is on wisdom and making wise choices. It's not about answering questions or decisions. It's not about whether something is good or bad, or right or wrong. Those are clearly important—but not the most important.

The opening quote in this chapter was written by King Solomon, considered to be the wisest man who ever lived. I have found it helpful to read what he has written. You can find his work in the Bible. Proverbs, Ecclesiastes, and Song of Solomon would be good places to start. At some point, I would highly recommend you also read more about his life. You have much to learn from the "wisest" man's life, including what not to do. Solomon started life strong but, over time, drifted so far that he never recovered.

If Solomon were alive today, I think he would enthusiastically endorse Andy's book, *Ask It.* It might have changed the trajectory of his life. Though my life started out poorly, I strive to stay on course to finish well. It's not easy. Thankfully, with resources like this book and asking "the question," I have the advantage of being aware of the importance of making *wise* choices.

I want the same for you. I want you to finish strong.

Go buy the book. You'll be glad you did!

# CHAPTER 14

# AFTER BROKENNESS

*We are all broken by something. We have all hurt someone and have been hurt. We all share the condition of brokenness even if our brokenness is not equivalent.*

—BRYAN STEVENSON

We are all broken, though not in the same ways. Ideally, our families should be the foundational source where we learn to love, care for, and support the people in our lives. Addressing brokenness is the first step toward living well-adjusted lives.

What we experience at home impacts us positively or negatively in ways we may not know or realize for many years. We share a universal desire to know who we are, where we fit in, and what will define us as individuals. Where and with whom we grow up influences our lives. The connections we make at home, school, church, and community contribute to our character development and values.

Our church in Orlando had a ministry called Men's Fraternity. During the summer, our pastor announced that on September 12, 2006, the fall session would run from 6 a.m. until

7:30 a.m. sharp. Meetings would be every Tuesday through to November 14. I now had an opportunity to be involved with other men.

On September 12, I got up early and drove to church. I arrived at 5:30 a.m., not knowing what to expect. I was amazed to see hundreds of men in the auditorium called Faith Hall. Seeing a hundred tables as I looked around the room caused anxiety to creep into my thoughts. Every table had ten chairs. If you just did the quick math, they expected one thousand men to show up that morning.

I immediately thought this was a mistake. I don't know anyone here. But then, one of the ushers observed me walking around aimlessly. He came over and introduced himself. Then, gesturing with his hand, he said seats aren't assigned and to take a seat anywhere.

I continued walking for a few minutes to see if I recognized anyone. It was a bit awkward. At that moment, I thought, *Just leave.* Then I saw a guy named Joel. He and his partners owned a physical therapy practice in Orlando. We recently met to discuss opportunities to work together. Our eyes connected. I was relieved, and Joel looked surprised. As I sat down, with a curious look, Joel said, "I didn't know you attended church here. What brought you to First Baptist?"

I told him about Jennifer's abduction and that my sister Joyce invited Debbie and me back in February. Joel and I became closer in the following weeks and years.

A few minutes later, Mike, a physical therapist who worked with Joel, sat down. *This is going to be okay.* Over time, I got to know Mike well. He was the PT for my daughter's high school soccer team and had treated Morgan several times. Not only was Mike a great physical therapist, but he was also a kind and caring man.

Men's Fraternity was about to begin. One of the facilitators drew our attention to the table signs with numbers. Our group of ten men became known as "table forty-six" for the next ten weeks. We studied Robert Lewis' *The Quest for Authentic Manhood* and tackled questions men struggle to understand. We learned how to be honest and vulnerable, discussing relational brokenness and the emotional wounds we carry. We discussed questions such as, "What makes a man, a man? A real man? Is there a moment when it happens? How should authentic manhood express itself today?" (Lewis 2003).

Over the next ten weeks, we unpacked our respective pasts, including our brokenness, by sharing vulnerably with the group. We discussed our relationships with our fathers, the power and importance of fathers modeling and raising healthy children, and our relationships with our spouses. We listened to each other and shed a few tears.

Each week the discussion topic was challenging. We faced the realities and quality of our relationships, especially with our fathers. I learned about myself and was thankful my dad and I were in a good place, having restored our relationship after several rough years.

I saw relationships through a new lens. It became clear and heartbreaking that I unintentionally created "wounds" that might result in brokenness in my children. The study provided the proper perspective. Our table discussions were priceless. Every man at our table offered unique insights from their relational experiences. And importantly, we prayed for each other to have the courage to continue making progress in our respective journeys.

With those insights, I scheduled time with my three children and apologized for not being the father and role model they deserved. I asked them to forgive me and promised to work hard to restore my relationship with them.

One morning, Pastor David announced that on Tuesday, November 14, our last meeting, they would be offering baptism to any man interested. I thought I'd pass since my parents baptized me as a baby.

Over the next week, during my prayer time, I felt the nudge to get baptized. *It's not for you. It's for your family. You're going public with what you believe.* The following Tuesday, I signed up to be baptized.

On Monday, November 13, I had a meeting in Ocala, Florida. Arriving early, I sat in the car and prayed. Then, while thinking about the baptism the next day, I heard, *Your prayer has been answered.* Those words took a few minutes to process. What did that mean? Suddenly, it hit me. I had prayed for God to take my life so Jenn could have hers back.

I couldn't believe it. God answered that prayer—differently than expected. Water immersion baptism symbolizes Jesus' death and resurrection. The following day, I would be submerged under water—a symbol of dying to self—and coming out of the water with a new life in Christ.

Our home was a beehive of activity at 4 a.m. on Tuesday, November 14. Showers, something to eat, and ready to get on the road to church by 5 a.m. Reese was pacing. She had no idea what was going on. She came and watched Debbie and me as we got dressed. Her tail wagged. At that moment, I turned to Debbie and said, "We can learn a lot by observing how our pets offer unconditional love. They just show up at the right times." It's ironic; I didn't even want a dog, but now we're walking buddies.

The morning's program was about to begin. Pastor David summarized our last eight weeks studying *The Quest for*

*Authentic Manhood.* He thanked God for the work He accomplished in all of us. Then, the baptisms began. Each man was introduced and asked to bring their table of guys with them and any family or friends. Pastor David introduced me and my family, Debbie, Nick, Morgan, Joyce, Drew, and Logan, then my table of forty-six guys, and finally, Bill Rush. He shared a brief background on my story and Jenn's abduction. I still remember Pastor David's words:

> *Bill's baptism this morning and commitment to*
> *Christ is evidence of Paul's words in Romans. "And*
> *we know that God causes everything to work*
> *together for the good of those who love God and*
> *are called according to his purpose for them." God*
> *did not cause what happened to Jennifer. But He*
> *did bring something good out of that tragedy—and*
> *we are witnesses of that good this morning.*

Before one thousand men, my family, and my friends, I celebrated my new life. Wow! Only God.

**REFLECTIONS**

As we touched on earlier: words matter. They will result in positive or negative consequences. The voices we hear are one thing, but the voices we choose to listen to are critical to the person we become. Our choice of words and tone can bring pain, discomfort, and brokenness. We might not have intended to create fallout, but it happens.

*In fact, there is a strength, a power even, in understanding brokenness, because embracing our brokenness creates a need and desire for mercy, and perhaps a corresponding need to show mercy. When you experience mercy, you learn things that are hard to learn otherwise. You see things you can't otherwise see; you hear things you can't otherwise hear. You begin to recognize the humanity that resides in each of us. All of a sudden, I felt stronger. I began thinking about what would happen if we all*

*just acknowledged our brokenness, if we owned up to*
*our weaknesses, our deficits, our biases, our fears.*

—BRYAN STEVENSON (STEVENSON 2014, 290-291)

Through our brokenness, we can move from *self-centered* individuals to people who are *other-focused.* Studying *The Quest for Authentic Manhood* brought understanding to my brokenness. I found hope in knowing God accepted me just as I was but loved me too much to leave me that way. Through His forgiveness, I experienced mercy and grace. My mission became clear. Inspire hope for the people in my life, starting with my wife and children.

The prophet Micah said:

*...the Lord has told you what is good, and this is what he requires of you: to do what is right, to love mercy, and to walk humbly with your God* (MICAH 6:8, NLT).

In our next chapter, we will read a powerful story of brokenness that resulted in a redeemed and transformed life that continues to impact thousands of people.

CHAPTER 15

# AFTER PRISON

*I've missed more than 9,000 shots in my career. I've lost almost 300 games. Twenty-six times I've been trusted to take the game winning shot and missed. I've failed over and over and over again in my life. And that is why I succeed.*

—MICHAEL JORDAN

Michael Jordan's quote reminds us failure is part of life if we try something new or practice to improve in a sport, hobby, skill, or activity. No one is perfect, and perfection shouldn't be the goal. Failure doesn't have to be the final word or a label attached to us.

Our successes may momentarily bring us happiness, but as we have discussed, happiness should not be our goal. In our failures, we learn the most valuable life lessons. We are humbled and reminded of how much more we need to know and learn.

From my experience, fully grasping and embracing the lessons failures teach requires being authentic and vulnerable. Refusing to ignore our present realities will impede our growth and maturity. As a result, drifting will likely occur, leading to isolation from the people we value most in our lives.

As I researched the importance of relational connections for this book, I came across Marcus Bullock, the founder and

CEO of Flikshop. This mobile app company developed a tool to help incarcerated people connect with families. I watched several podcasts and read as much as possible for background and context (Bullock 2019, 2020, 2021).

His story emphasizes the importance of family, faith, and unconditional love. These bonds keep us connected, supported, and encouraged. They give us hope during extremely challenging moments in our lives.

Born in Hyattsville, Maryland, Marcus' father left the family when he was two years old, leaving his mother, Sylvia, and sister, Melanie. His mother worked for the Food and Drug Administration while attending college to support her family.

Sylvia placed high importance on being a good role model for her kids and stressed the value of getting an education and the importance of community. So, she moved into an apartment building in the same District of Columbia complex as her aunt. Unfortunately, drugs overtook neighborhoods in the 1980s and early 1990s, and murders were reported on the news daily. A few blocks away, people were openly selling drugs.

Sylvia knew she had to keep Melanie and Marcus connected to a community. Their church was an essential part of her plan. They were in the kid's choir, participated in Bible studies, and attended prayer services.

As a young teen, Marcus was an honor student and a good basketball player with aspirations of playing in the NBA. Most of his friends were from church or elementary and middle school.

Marcus described his mother as a wise spender: "She would not spend more than fifty dollars for a pair of tennis shoes. Growing up in an era of Air Jordans, that was impossible." He knew to get the Jordans, he'd have to earn the money.

The entrepreneurial spirit was in Marcus. His first business was buying a bag of Blow Pops at the local grocery store and selling them for twenty-five cents each. On his first day, he sold out before getting off the bus. He began to fill a jar with the money. His mom was thrilled the "entrepreneur bug" had bitten him, so she encouraged him. He bought his own Jordans. Unfortunately, Marcus was about to have a pivotal moment, a moment most of us cannot even fathom.

In 1994, Marcus turned thirteen and had just returned home from a church event one evening, still wearing his full suit and dress shoes. Melanie asked him to go to their aunt's home to borrow her iron. As he was walking home from his aunt's building, he passed some guys on the street corner, greeted them, and continued walking, aware a car had been slowly following him.

Suddenly, one of the passengers in the vehicle asked him, "Where does Candy live?"

Marcus told them, "There is no girl by that name in the neighborhood."

The guy persisted, "She lives in building 1956."

Marcus turned toward the building and realized it was 1956. As he turned back toward the car, he came face to face with a gun pointed at him. The guy holding the gun told him not to scream.

Marcus said, "My heart dropped. I screamed, 'Holy crap. Are you going to kill me?'" Marcus then got pushed into the car's back seat, and it took off.

These guys saw him out at night and assumed he was selling drugs. They drove around for hours and began peppering him with questions about drugs, money, and if he owned a safe. Marcus thought his life was over. He told them, "I don't have any money. I don't have a safe."

"Take us to your house," they told him.

Marcus thought about his mom and sister at home and told them, "No."

Meanwhile, his mom called her aunt and was surprised Marcus was not with her. Now she was worried about what had happened to him.

For the second time, Marcus had a gun pointed at his head. The guy holding the gun said, "If we let you go, you never saw us or the gun, right?"

Marcus nervously replied, "If you let me go. I'll never ever, ever call the police. I don't even know what you look like."

The car stopped. He got out and started running for home, still in his dress shoes and suit and holding the iron for his sister. Marcus thought, *What in the world just happened?*

He walked into his home, drenched with sweat and crying. After hearing from Marcus what happened, his mother was in shock, trying to grasp the seriousness of the situation.

Hearing Marcus tell his story caused me to have a visceral response. It felt like the night my sister Joyce told me Jennifer was missing. Those emotions are raw and overwhelming. Night after night, you watch the evening news. You're in disbelief hearing about the awful things people do to one another. One day you go from watching the news to being a news story.

That night, Marcus decided he needed protection. At thirteen years old, he lived in a situation most of us can't imagine. The fact that buying a gun was his first choice is surreal. When he left the house, he took his keys and the gun every day. Then, at night, he hid it under his mattress so his mother couldn't find it.

My first thoughts were the words on a framed placard on a wall in our family room. It was Dorothy Law Nolte's "children learn what they live." Marcus lived in a hostile environment, so his fight reflex kicked in.

Sylvia noticed Marcus became angrier. He started spending time with older guys, doing what they were doing. One of the guys was Big Mike. He always had his pit bull by his side. In Marcus' mind, Big Mike and his pit bull represented what a man's man should look like, a picture of masculinity. Marcus wanted to be like Big Mike. One day, he was hanging out and getting high. Big Mike talked about selling crack. Marcus asked him, "What do you have to do? Big Mike told Marcus, "Drugs sell themselves. You literally stand outside on a corner and wait for someone to approach you." Big Mike explained the economics of selling drugs, and Marcus' entrepreneurial mind kicked in. It was easy making money with candy. He could make more money selling drugs. This is another surreal moment. Marcus was getting high with Big Mike, and his thirteen-year-old brain began to imagine his future as a millionaire.

One of his church friends, Kevin, lived in a neighborhood known for selling drugs. Kevin introduced Marcus to a guy he could buy drugs from. With an initial investment of $125 from candy profits, Marcus began making nearly one thousand dollars per week.

His mother, busy with work and college, had no idea what he was doing. Marcus was living a double life, keeping up appearances at church and grades in school.

Eventually, Marcus lost interest in the drug business. He wanted to make money faster. One day while talking to friends, they discussed stealing cars. It was much riskier than standing on a corner selling drugs. But a friend told them they could make five thousand dollars stealing cars. The entrepreneurial wheels turned.

In 1995, Marcus turned fourteen and was excited to make more money stealing cars. Friends told him how to do it. He already knew how to drive. He had taken his mom's car and drove his sister around the neighborhood. In his community, stealing cars was part of everyday life. Behind one of the apartment buildings was an area used to park stolen cars.

Marcus recalled the first car he stole. After a few tries, he got the ignition assembly out and used a flathead screwdriver to start the vehicle. In fewer than sixty seconds, he made five thousand dollars. Becoming a millionaire was in view.

It's hard to fully comprehend the living environment in which all of this is happening. It echoes the aforementioned quote by Fyodor Dostoevsky about lying to ourselves and believing the lies, so it's impossible to see reality.

Marcus lived two different lives. Stealing cars while attending church, Bible studies, and basketball practice, as well as keeping his grades up and remaining on the honor roll.

In 1996, Marcus turned fifteen. One of his best friends, Dwayne, struggled to understand life's meaning and purpose. They were both in the math club and tutors for other students. Both played basketball and wanted to be NBA players. Their conversations centered around basketball, girls, ambitions, and sometimes the next crime Marcus would commit.

Then, one day, Dwayne said he wanted to learn how to steal a car. A couple of weeks later, they were ready to work together. Marcus believed stealing cars was a way to make a million dollars. He dreamed of going to Duke University and playing for the Chicago Bulls. This delusional thinking expanded to include believing all the good things he was doing at church and in school would outweigh his criminal activity.

Christmas season was approaching. Marcus and Dwayne decided to go to a mall in northern Virginia, where it would be easier to steal a more expensive car. Dwayne had a screwdriver, but Marcus brought his gun. Walking through the parking lot, they saw a man sleeping in a car. They tapped the window with the gun and startled the guy. They told him to get out of his car. Dwayne jumped into the driver's seat, and Marcus into the passenger seat. As they left, they laughed and joked around. Then they saw the man's credit cards and went shopping at Pentagon City Mall.

Bad decision after bad decision. A cashier asked about the name on the credit card and got on the phone for verification. Marcus and Dwayne's hearts raced, and their palms were sweating. Dwayne noticed a security guard approaching, so they took off running for the car.

Police sirens blared as Marcus and Dwayne drove toward an office building. It turned out to be the Pentagon. Helicopters are now overhead. The police closed in, and they were both arrested and charged with carjacking, attempted robbery, kidnapping, and firearm use in the commission of a felony.

## THE IMPACT OF CHOICES

Choices. We make countless decisions a day. Yet, how often do we consider the consequences or the potential collateral damage that might result from our actions and decisions?

While writing this, I'm thinking, *How does a fifteen-year-old honor student, a promising basketball player, and an active member of his church wind up in jail, charged with a felony?*

Andy Stanley's quote in *The Principle of the Path: How to Get from Where You Are to Where You Want to Be* offers a glimpse:

> *Direction—not intention—determines our destination.*
> *The direction you are currently traveling...will determine*

*where you end up. This is true regardless of your goals, your dreams, your wishes, or your wants…Just as there are paths that have led us to places we never intended to be, there are paths that lead us away from those places as well* (STANLEY 2008, 14–15).

Marcus and Dwayne committed the crimes they were charged with. They never intended to hurt anyone. After all, they were teenagers. In their community, this was what excitement looked like.

Unfortunately, laws had changed. They both were charged as adults and faced possible life sentences. They opted to accept plea agreements. As a result, Marcus was sentenced to eight years and Dwayne to nine years since he drove the car. They would serve their sentences in a maximum-security prison.

Remember, Marcus was an honor student, good at math, and a tutor, and he had the entrepreneurial bug. One day on the prison basketball court, he met Tony, who had been sentenced to fourteen years for armed robberies, conspiracy to deliver controlled substances, and weapons charges. Tony came from the DC area, so with that in common, he became a big brother to Marcus. Other prisoners noticed Marcus was articulate and asked him for help writing letters to their families and setting up their commissary accounts.

In 1998, Marcus turned seventeen. He noticed guys were buying food at the commissary, devouring everything quickly. His entrepreneurial spirit ignited. He realized he could purchase honey buns and hold onto them. In the middle of the month, when people wanted food, he would sell them one honeybun for two honeybuns from their next commissary visit. After a few months, he had hundreds of honey buns. The profits allowed him to send money home to help his mother. His business was a way to escape the reality of prison. However, isolation took a toll on him. With hundreds of men in his facility, he only saw Dwayne a few times walking through hallways. Anger set in, leading to outbursts and fighting, which resulted in solitary confinement.

## A MOTHER'S UNCONDITIONAL LOVE

When Sylvia learned Marcus was spiraling out of control, she visited him. "Marcus, I'm not going to let you get caught up in the prison culture. I'm going to write you a letter or send you a picture every day for the next six years so you can understand there is life after prison. This is not the end. I believe God has set you down so he can stand you up."

True to her word, a couple of days later, Marcus received letters and photos from his mother. He looked forward to getting mail. Finally, Marcus pulled out of his depression and realized those letters and pictures helped him and his friends. Staying connected to his family and community encouraged him.

## OPPORTUNITY TO LEARN

Marcus turned twenty-one. After serving six years of his sentence, the Brunswick Correctional Center started offering classes on business computer software applications. Marcus wanted to learn how to create something. He decided to take courses to provide better opportunities when he got home.

On February 4, 2004, now twenty-three, Marcus was released from prison. His mother and sister were waiting to welcome him.

Marcus had new goals and a purpose. He wanted to be a businessman. However, he would face significant obstacles in pursuing his new path. Every job application asked, "Have you ever been convicted of a felony?" He had to check yes. However, on his forty-second job interview, he was handed an application, but that felony question was different. There was a *comma*. Have you ever been convicted of a felony comma in the last seven years? Finally, he didn't have to check the box.

He began working in a paint store. Listening to and observing customers, he often heard them ask how much the store charged to do a painting job. The store didn't offer painting services. His entrepreneurial spirit kicked in once again. He created a business called Prospectus Painting Contractors.

### INSPIRING HOPE AND HELPING OTHERS

Marcus wanted to give back to help others just like his mother had done for him. Getting mail from family on a regular basis helped during his transition home. Many of his friends remained incarcerated, and he wanted them to stay connected through pictures and letters.

With the software application training he had received, Marcus decided to build a mobile app that could take photos, upload them, and add a message. He would print them on a postcard and ship them to anyone in any cell, anywhere in the country. The company he started was called Flikshop. The company website says,

> *Each one of our Flikshop postcards are filled with words of love, emojis, confessions of yearning, and some pain. They tell a story, and our founder Marcus Bullock knew that*

*we needed to figure out a way to leverage this love to help end recidivism around the globe. We want every person in every cell to have mail every day.* (FLIKSHOP).

Realizing the importance of the skills training he received in prison, Marcus and his team created the Flikshop School of Business. The "About Us" page on the company website says:

*Entrepreneurship has been a proven strategy for mentoring, training, and preparing for the workforce. We introduce every student to a curriculum...to build confidence, learn strategy and communication skills, and how to plan for a life of entrepreneurship.* (FLIKSHOP SCHOOL OF BUSINESS).

## REFLECTIONS

Failure did not have the last word in Marcus' life. He is encouraging families and offering hope to millions of people in prisons all over the country.

Despite his success, Marcus said his most significant accomplishment was going to his office. He describes,

I see that selfie of a kindergartner along with the text that says, "Hey Dad, I love you, and I miss you." And it's printed on a postcard that we're getting ready to ship to his cell.

Matthew recorded Jesus' words about caring for the least of us, "I needed clothes and you clothed me, I was sick and you looked after me, I was in prison and you came to visit me." (Matthew 25:36, NIV).

You and I may not be able to visit prisons, but we can support the work of Flikshop!

I wanted to punctuate Marcus' powerful story of life transformation with Thomas Edison's words as the exclamation point:

> *Surprises and reverses can serve as an incentive for great accomplishment. There are no rules here, we're just trying to accomplish something.*
>
> —THOMAS EDISON (EDISON AND BEALS 1997)

# CHAPTER 16

# AFTER SUICIDE

*Grief is like a long valley, a winding valley where*
*any bend may reveal a totally new landscape.*

—C. S. LEWIS

During our Saturday, February 16, 2008, service, we learned Jeremy, our teaching pastor, Dr. Jimmy Knott's son, had taken his life on Wednesday. Our church family grieved with Jimmy, his wife Linda, their children, Jeremy's wife Lorena, and their young daughter Alyssa.

At the time, Debbie and I had attended First Baptist Orlando for two years. We experienced this church family's love and support after Jenn's abduction. We looked forward to being present and praying for Jimmy and his family.

We cannot imagine the pain, grief, and sense of loss in one of the most heart-wrenching situations anyone must endure. So how do you process the swirling emotions when someone you love takes their own life?

As a pastor, having experienced unspeakable tragedy, he knew his pain could be of assistance to other people. What Jimmy now felt gave him insight into the stigma that suicide creates. He understood feeling isolated, shame, guilt, denial, and anger. These emotions contribute to shutting public discussion on the topic.

Barbara Beck, with Good Life Orlando, invited Pastor Jimmy and Linda to share their story to offer hope to families living in the aftermath of a suicide (Beck 2013).

Jimmy and Linda talked about how Jeremy had struggled academically with attention deficit and debilitating migraines from a young age so badly he would curl up in a ball to escape the pain. After being prescribed Ritalin, Jeremy flourished in school and improved his grades. However, after entering high school, he didn't like how the medicine made him feel and chose to self-medicate. He began drinking alcohol and using controlled substances, leading to bad decisions with severe consequences.

One day, a church staff member who had drug rehabilitation experience crossed paths with Jeremy. They bonded, and the gentleman offered to help him. He told Jeremy, "If you will listen to me, I'll get you through this." Jeremy agreed and would spend time in an in-house rehab facility.

He turned the corner, became a successful real estate agent, and loved his new career. Jeremy met and married Lorena, a positive influence in his life. They had a child together, Alyssa, who adored her father.

During the market collapse in 2008, Jeremy lost everything, including their home and car. So, he and his family moved in with Jimmy and Linda. Things seemed to be okay. Then, a couple of weeks before he died, Jeremy wanted peace with God, so he asked his parents for some material to read. On the day he died, he turned back to alcohol, returned to their old house, now abandoned, and took his life.

Until then, no one saw any apparent signs or clues that Jeremy would do something drastic. But Jimmy said, "If it happened after three or four bad years, it might not have been so surprising, but for where he was and what was going on, we were very surprised."

Jimmy talked about suicide impacting many more families than we could imagine. After their loss, people Jimmy worked with or knew began to share their stories of losing a loved one to suicide. What amazed Jimmy was he had known many of these people for years and never knew the grief they had been carrying.

So, he decided to do some research to understand the issue better. Jimmy shared staggering numbers: "About every forty seconds in America, someone attempts suicide. That boils down to somebody succeeding and committing suicide every fifteen minutes."

The Centers for Disease Control and Prevention (CDC) reports that suicide is a leading cause of death and a serious public health problem. In 2020 an estimated 12.2 million American adults seriously thought about suicide. The aftermath of individuals who commit suicide and/or attempt suicide affects the emotional, economic, physical, health, and well-being of many people connected with them. Many will experience feelings of shock, anger, guilt, and depression. The CDC emphasized suicide is preventable. However, everyone has a role in "creating healthy and strong individuals, families, and communities" (CDC 2022).

Jimmy said, "When a perfect storm of terrible circumstances came together, triggered by alcohol, Jeremy made a life-altering decision that impacted our family for the rest of our lives."

They found truth and comfort in the words from Corrie Ten Boom's book, *The Hiding Place,* as she leaned down to make out Betsie's words: "...must tell people that there is no pit so deep that He is not deeper still. They will listen to us, Corrie, because we have been here" (Boom et al. 2015).

For Linda, surviving each day was a challenge. She spent more time reading her Bible and being alone with God. The passages comforted her, and walking was therapeutic. Linda was encouraged by the support of many people. She and her family were not alone.

Jimmy said, "We've discovered in our experience and then watching others grieve is one of the hardest things we are called to do. It's going to happen to all of us. But it's been a great journey learning about grief. I think everybody finds their grief groove, their rhythm. It's going to be very different. You can't rush it."

Jimmy was thankful this experience made him more sensitive and caring about other people's pain. As a pastor, he said, "I was brought to a deeper dependency on the Lord, and the work of His Spirit in my life, which I desperately needed."

Jimmy and Linda had a lot of questions about Jeremy's suicide. However, they made a distinction between asking questions *of* God versus questioning God. "We never questioned God; He makes no mistakes. He is perfectly good. We live in a fallen world. We make bad decisions, and the people we know and love make bad decisions that dramatically affect those who love them."

As the interview ended, Barbara asked Jimmy to share some final thoughts from his heart that might help someone experiencing similar pain.

He thanked her and said, "A couple of things are fresh in my mind. The first thing I'd say is unspeakable tragedy always presents an unbelievable opportunity. We're all going to face difficulties and tragedies, the intensity may vary, but they're very painful to the person walking through them."

Jimmy offered, "Despite the circumstances we may find ourselves in, no matter the difficulty, always make the right choice. Our response is the only thing we are in control of." Looking straight into the camera, Jimmy said:

*The second thing I want to remind us of is we live in a world that is always seeking explanations. What we need to rely on are solutions. And I will tell you Christ is the solution. There is joy in this life, and there's comfort in this life, no matter the difficulty we face. And there is hope for the next. So, hold on. God will be with you regardless of the difficulty and storm that you face.*

## FINDING TANGIBLE HOPE
*Experiencing grief does not indicate a loss of faith. When a person of deep faith loses someone, it's important to remember that grief is about their own experience of loss. It's perfectly reasonable for someone to believe that their loved one is in a better place, and still to feel overwhelmed with the pain of being separated from them.*

—LITSA WILLIAMS (WILLIAMS 2014)

In early January 2016, I received a call from a friend, Terry Myers. We met soon after moving to Richmond in April 2013. Terry, a workers' compensation claims adjuster, and I worked on a case together. When she received my email, she noticed something different with my signature: "Please pray for my niece, Jennifer Kesse, abducted and missing since 2006." So, she called to ask me about Jennifer.

Terry and her husband, Chuck, lived in Orlando and were familiar with Jenn's abduction. They were long-time members of First Baptist Orlando. They remembered when Pastor David would have Joyce and Drew come before the congregation for prayer and encouragement. Talk about a small world. We both agreed there were no coincidences. We became friends and frequently got together, and they joined a Bible study we hosted in our home.

Many years ago, beginning in November, First Baptist Orlando asked the congregation to pray for a *word* representing something God may want to work on in our lives in the new year. Our pastors would begin by sharing their "words" in late December. On the last Sunday of 2015, Pastor Jimmy shared a message on his word for 2016: hope (First Baptist Church - Orlando 2015).

The next day an excited Terry called. "Did you watch Jimmy's message yesterday?"

"No," I replied, "haven't gotten to watch it yet."

Terry emphatically said, "You must watch it, and soon. You'll know why at the end of the message. And you have to share this with Joyce and Drew."

"If it's that important, I'll watch the service as soon as we hang up," I committed. And I did.

Her excitement became obvious at the end of Jimmy's message. He shared a detail, a tangible answer to prayer—an answer like the one I had received in December 2007.

Pastor Jimmy stated that Biblical hope is a certainty. The Old and New Testaments have approximately one-hundred and eighty references to hope. If you looked at the word usage, Jimmy suggested we could insert words such as "trust" or "promise." So, Biblical hope is a confident expectation. Everything God promises will happen.

In his message, Jimmy said, "Hope is God's gift; hope is God's plan" for everyone in this life. He and his family anchored themselves to hope after Jeremy passed away. In those dark days, they felt hopeless. Jimmy and Linda started journaling what was happening in their hearts and minds. Linda wrote extensively about her experience openly, which fit well with Jimmy's word for the year, hope.

In her journal, Linda was honest in writing what she experienced. For three years, her constant companions were insomnia, depression, and a broken heart. She reminded herself often that Jesus heals the brokenhearted. That promise gave her peace. Linda immersed herself in scripture, writing down verses that spoke of God's love and care for her. Praying was challenging because fatigue impacted her ability to focus. Part of Linda's daily routine included walking and often praying at Woodlawn Memorial Garden. She wrote out a prayer she would read every day.

Finally, one morning, Linda woke up, realizing she had slept all night. Overjoyed at the possibility of not being continually tired, she went for a walk filled with praise for a restful night. She said, "I'm actually thinking straight for a change." Remembering Bible verses and knowing God is a God of hope, she said, "I want to feel joy and peace so that I might abound in hope."

Linda walked past a tree and saw something reflecting light from a spot where a limb was missing. As she approached the tree, she observed something shiny. Looking closer, it was a metal object with letters. As she grasped it, she was surprised. It was the word *hope*.

Linda said, "My prayer changed. You've got to be kidding me. God, it can't be. You put a message in a tree for me! I went home and explained to Jimmy I'd found hope and I'll never lose it again. I carried it around in my purse for a year, and now it lives under my pillow. I know it's just a piece of metal. But it reminds me of a very mighty God."

Jimmy concluded by saying, "So, is there any hope? You bet there is, but not hope so, but hope *know* because it is certain because it's based on the character of a faithful God."

**REFLECTIONS**

Terry was right. Linda's experience and my experience were similar. Only God can provide tangible hope in unexpected ways. In chapter ten, I shared how God demonstrated His love, concern, and compassion to me. That heart-shaped pendant and Linda's metal word *hope* continue to provide daily reminders that God knows our hearts' desires and meets us where we are.

The COVID-19 global pandemic impacted everyone to some degree. However, students were particularly affected by a shift from an in-person to a virtual learning environment.

According to a CDC report, "[d]isruptions and consequences related to the COVID-19 pandemic, including school closures, social isolation, family economic hardship, family loss or illness, and reduced access to health care, raise concerns about their effects on the mental health and well-being of youths" (CDC 2022).

If you know someone potentially at risk, reach out to an appropriate person or organization for guidance and support. The Suicide and Crisis Lifeline is 988. Additional resources are available on the CDC website.

No one is immune from the effects of uncertainty. Watching the news and living life provides evidence of financial, relational, career, and health challenges. They seem to swirl around us continually.

The result? Feelings of helplessness and hopelessness can quickly overwhelm us, clouding reasonable judgment. We may seek counseling, prayer, and support from others, but we need *hope.*

Regardless of what you may face, keep your hearts and minds open. Allow family and friends to be present for you, to listen, and to offer hugs.

From the very beginning of God's story, He tells us that He walked and talked with Adam and Eve. He is the same God today, seeking after you, wanting to walk and talk with you. He wants to give you hope—a confident hope. He is with you right now, just start talking and then pause to listen quietly.

Paul of Tarsus experienced pain and suffering. He was beaten and left for dead—shipwrecked and bitten by a deadly poisonous snake and countless other trials and tests. Yet Paul knew where his hope was anchored. Writing to followers of Jesus in Rome experiencing persecution, he said, "May the God of hope fill you with all joy and peace in believing, so by the power of the Holy Spirit you may abound in hope" (Romans 15:13, ESV).

Jimmy declared, "If you are breathing, you need encouragement and hope. May everyone seek and possess the hope that only God can offer."

PART FIVE

# FAITH IN ACTION

CHAPTER 17

# DONATING LIFE

*I never used to pay that much attention to organ donation,*
*but I'm tremendously glad for it: it turned out that I*
*was one of the ones in need. I hope my donor's family*
*will be blessed a thousand times for their sacrifice.*

—KARL BLACK

Imagine one day you feel perfectly healthy and, seemingly overnight, you know something isn't right. You feel tired and washed out and don't know why. So you go to the doctor, have some tests, and then receive devastating news. Your kidneys aren't working. What? How do you process that information? You ask the doctor what's the plan and find out you'll be starting dialysis immediately. Dialysis will remove the toxins from your body until a kidney becomes available for transplantation.

## PRAYING FOR A DONOR

I was looking forward to Monday, September 14, 2015. That was going to be my first night leading a group of men in Bible study in Richmond, Virginia. Previously, I had served as a children's leader in the Orlando evening men's class. Adding to the excitement, Bible Study Fellowship had just introduced a new study for the year, Revelation. That night, I met the guys who would be part of the group for the next nine months. We had a great group of men of varying ages, business, and cultural backgrounds. An essential part of our men's groups is praying for each other.

One of the guys, Bill Weatherford, has been a member of the Richmond class for years. Always a gentleman, reserved, and thoughtful. He was the last person to respond. In a low voice, he said, "I would appreciate it if you all would pray for my wife, MJ (Mary Jane). Her kidneys completely shut down. It was totally unexpected. She's going to need a kidney donor."

We all looked at each other, surprised at his request's seriousness. Then, we all responded out loud that we would pray. When I sent the prayer requests by email, I wrote, "Pray for a *suitable* donor for MJ."

My only familiarity with organ donation was checking the box on a form at the motor vehicle office. They would add a designation on my driver's license. However, I would soon learn much more about the process and the benefit for the recipient of a living organ donation.

Every Monday night, Bill would provide an update on how MJ was doing and if there was progress in identifying a donor. In one update, Bill shared he had gone through the initial testing process but was not a match. Week after week, Bill's demeanor had an air of disappointment and frustration with how complex the process was.

Without a doubt, waiting is challenging and can be discouraging. However, our men's group kept encouraging him to be patient. God was working on a *suitable* donor.

We ended our first study semester in early December. Bill reported several people had volunteered to go through the testing process, but no one was a match. At this point there were no potential donors in the queue. We all agreed to continue to pray for a *suitable* donor over the Christmas holiday.

One morning in the first week of January 2016, I was praying for MJ and heard a clear prompting to volunteer to be screened as a possible donor. That morning I called Bill and told him I wanted to meet to discuss what I needed to do. We agreed to meet for a coffee a couple of days later.

Bill brought a brochure from HCA Virginia Transplant Center at Henrico Doctor's Hospital in Richmond, Virginia. It provided good information and the contact number to schedule an appointment.

I called the transplant center and spoke with Melissa Van Syckle, RN, the living donor coordinator. After a brief conversation, we scheduled an initial interview for the following week.

On the day of the appointment, I felt peace and excitement that I might be a match for MJ. While driving to the HCA Transplant Center, I listened to the local K-Love radio station. Just as I was about to cross the James River, the radio host shared a story of a young couple who married about a year ago. Soon after the wedding, the wife went into kidney failure. She needed a transplant. Her new husband went through the evaluation process and was a match. With a pause, the host said he was a hundred pounds overweight, so he was not approved because of the health risk. Out of love for his new bride, her husband decided to lose a hundred pounds so he could donate a kidney to his wife. The radio host said the surgeries went well, and both quickly recovered.

I immediately glanced up and said, "I got this, Lord. I'm all in on this." At that moment, I knew I'd be a match.

My initial meeting with Melissa Van Syckle went well. She was personable, knowledgeable, and professional. With years of experience, she confidently presented an overview of the living donor program and how the process worked. Melissa emphasized that protecting the donor's health was the primary focus of the evaluation process.

She shared some staggering national statistics about the need for kidney donors. The National Kidney Foundation (www. kidney.org) reported that one in three Americans are at risk for kidney disease. Thirty-seven million people have chronic kidney disease. Over six hundred thousand people live with kidney failure. Finally, Melissa said over a hundred thousand patients are waiting for a kidney transplant on any given day.

Considering the problem's complexity, identifying potential donors, and the time involved in the evaluation process, I learned some people wait four years for life-saving transplants. Some much longer. Importantly, recipients do much better with a living kidney donation.

I was overwhelmed by the numbers. One of them now had a name, MJ. It was personal. I asked Melissa why you don't see TV commercials promoting awareness. She said the National Kidney Foundation and a Richmond-based group, Donate Life, do what they can to help get the word out.

We then got to an early first hurdle. I would turn sixty in a few months. Typically, older donors have preexisting conditions that automatically rule them out. Top of the list is high blood pressure. Melissa asked if I had been diagnosed with hypertension. I said, "Yes."

That got Melissa's attention, and she quickly asked, "What medication are you taking?"

"Cozaar," I replied. Melissa relaxed and looked relieved. It turns out Cozaar is on the approved list because it doesn't impact kidney function, and it has protective properties for the kidneys.

Melissa described the next steps in some detail. First, living donors have no financial risk because Medicare pays for all the costs associated with the donation process. She had prepared paperwork and forms for me to fill out and said this process could take a couple of months due to the coordination of schedules.

On the table was a poster for a program called Kidney Paired Exchange. I asked what it was. Melissa explained that sometimes a potential donor, like me, is an acceptable match but not perfect according to how they score donors and recipients. The national registry compiles all the patient data from donors and recipients, regularly scanning to find the best matches. This process gives the recipient the best chance of a successful transplant. If I was a match for MJ, this would be an option. The process had started.

As I was driving home, something I heard years earlier popped into my thoughts. It was something Andy Stanley said: "Do for one what you wish you could do for everyone" (Stanley 2019).

When I considered the statistics, I wanted to do more to promote the awareness and benefits of living donation. But, at the time, my life was busy. I didn't know where to begin. However, this chapter is that opportunity.

The medical screening started quickly. First up was completing an extensive personal health history questionnaire about me, my parents, and my siblings. Asking all the questions you can imagine. Based on my health history, the next step was to have several vials of blood drawn. Next was a urine sample, followed by an electrocardiogram and x-ray of my lungs. Everything was good so far.

Next up was a kidney function test. And after that was an abdominal CT scan that took images from the neck to the pelvis. Melissa explained they needed to determine the size, structure, and position of my kidneys and my vascular system. A few more appointments remained. One was with a psychologist who would evaluate my emotional well-being. An essential part of the process. It ensured I was mentally prepared for the surgery, focusing on what-ifs. What if the recipient (MJ) doesn't do well or dies due to the surgery or soon after? What if I experienced health issues after surgery? I wasn't worried, but this made perfect sense to me.

We were nearing the end of the process. A team of medical specialists would review my results and eligibility to be a living donor for MJ. Then we waited.

One morning, Melissa called to tell me I was a match for MJ. But she paused, saying I was not the best match. The opportunity for the best match would happen if we both agreed to enroll in the Kidney Paired Exchange national registry. We agreed.

I remember the night Bill and I shared the news with our men's group. We thanked God for providing a *suitable* donor. That night, our prayers changed to, "Lord, provide MJ with the *perfect* match."

Unfortunately, the transplant coordinators could not predict when the best match for MJ would happen. Now we had to wait on the process to work.

## CONTROL IS PAINFUL

*Pain insists upon being attended to. God whispers to us in our pleasures, speaks in our consciences, but shouts in our pains: it is His megaphone to rouse a deaf world.*

—C.S. LEWIS (LEWIS 1940)

I learned God had other plans for me as all this was happening. He had a new assignment in the Richmond BSF class. The longtime teaching leader for this class would retire in May 2016 at the end of the class year.

One morning in late February, while in New Jersey, I received a call from Ken. After a few minutes of catching up, he said, "I would like you to prayerfully consider becoming the next teaching leader for the Richmond class." Of course, I was honored to be considered and said I would pray.

I immediately called my former teaching leader, Ed Wood, in the Orlando class. I told him about the call and asked if he and the group of men in Orlando would pray for me. He agreed and encouraged me, saying, "Based on what I've been observing, God has been at work preparing you and planning for this new assignment for some time. I'd be honored to pray for you."

Ultimately, I accepted that role and traveled to San Antonio, Texas, in April for training. However, upon returning, I began to experience some anxiety. My mind focused on the upcoming commitments. An uncertain surgery date and planning for a new role at BSF. How was I going to manage to get everything accomplished?

Waiting had never been one of my best character traits. And worse, I had no control over the kidney donation process. So, rather than trusting God to work everything out, I began praying. "God, if possible, would you provide the perfect donor for MJ? I'd like to have the surgery as soon as possible. Before August would be great."

You may think I'm making this up, but I'm not. That was my request to God. The same God who prompted me to donate a kidney, ensured the screening process was successful, and called me to a new role in BSF. But, because my plans were more important, I'm treating Him like my personal assistant, handling meeting schedules and my calendar. Unbelievable.

Just off the mountain top of excitement, down to the valley of discouragement over a situation and timing I couldn't control.

We planned a family vacation the week before Memorial Day on Long Beach Island in New Jersey. We were gathering to celebrate my sixtieth birthday. While loading the car, I lifted one of the suitcases and twisted. Pain shot through my lower back. Up to this moment, I had never had any back issues. During the drive up from Florida, the discomfort increased. When we arrived at the beach house, the pain was bad enough that I couldn't help unload the car. Throughout the week, the pain persisted, but I managed.

The drive home was tolerable. However, after arriving home, I could barely get out of bed. The pain was so bad. The doctor prescribed a prednisone pack and pain relievers to get me through the acute phase until I could see a specialist, which wasn't until late June.

At that appointment, I was given options based on the MRI results and decided to schedule an epidural injection. Unfortunately, the earliest available appointment was in late August. Yikes. So much for wanting to have my entire life organized so that everything would go according to *my* plans.

I called Melissa to let her know what was happening since I wasn't sure how my current situation might impact the process. I then called Bill and MJ to let them know. They were wonderful. They had a wedding in August, so any potential delay worked for them. They both said they would be praying for me.

During this entire time, my conversations with God went something like this: "I don't get this, God. I'm serving you in BSF and in my church. I did what you asked; I'm donating a kidney to MJ. So why am I experiencing this back pain? Why is this happening? I don't get this."

In hindsight, my complaining lasted much longer than it should have. I had been walking with God for nearly ten years. I knew better. But my plans and desire for control proved to be very painful.

One day I called a friend who was also a spiritual mentor from Florida, Jay Fernandez. He patiently listened to my story and complaints. Then, without missing a beat, Jay said, "Sounds like you're trying to control the situation. You know who is in control, right?" Jay followed up with, "Why are you asking God 'why' questions? Stop asking why and ask God to reveal what He wants to teach you in this situation." Jay was right. Yet I felt so foolish at that moment. Self-centeredness has a way of bringing the worst out of us.

I quickly forgot God's many blessings over the past ten years. I loved having those mountaintop experiences. The excitement of walking with God and serving Him and others. But when things didn't go as I planned, into the valley of despair, I went. Sadly, I stayed in that valley feeling sorry for myself, wishing things were different.

In his book *The Noticer: Sometimes, All a Person Needs Is a Little Perspective,* Andy Andrews discusses the challenges of our maturing faith:

> *Think with me here...everybody wants to be on the mountaintop, but if you'll remember, mountaintops are rocky and cold. There is no growth on the top of a mountain. Sure, the view is great, but what's a view for? A view just gives us a glimpse of our next destination— our next target. But to hit that target, we must come off the mountain, go through the valley, and begin to climb the next slope. It is in the valley that we*

*slog through the lush grass and rich soil, learning and*
*becoming what enables us to summit life's next peak.*

—ANDY ANDREWS (ANDREWS 2009, 8)

After my call with Jay, my conversations with God changed. First, I asked Him to forgive me for being selfish and not trusting Him. Then, I asked Him to let me know what He wanted me to learn from this experience. It didn't take long. God spoke clearly: "What have you been praying for, MJ? A perfect donor match, right? Stop trying to control everything. Let go and let me work everything out."

Wow! I needed that reminder. No matter how long I've been walking with God, it is never a question of if, but rather when I'm going to walk off the path or fall into a ditch. God knew all of this was going to happen. He was right next to me, walking through it with me.

I was there for them when my children struggled, got rebellious, and drifted. I wasn't happy about their behaviors or choices, but that didn't change my love for them. And it didn't change God's love for me.

I love the way King David—yes, the same one who took on Goliath—spoke about God: "You have examined my heart and know everything about me. You know when I sit down or stand up...you know everything I do. You know what I am going to say even before I say it" (Psalm 139:1-4, NLT).

David recognized a truth I had to acknowledge. God knows everything about me. Nothing takes Him by surprise. My primary responsibility must be to trust, listen, and obey what He asks. I had to let go of what I don't understand and stop focusing on the outcome.

Day by day, my back began improving. Debbie suggested I go with her to a barre class at our fitness center. Taking the classes helped her manage back pain for many years. I agreed to go. It turned out to be a wise decision. I improved enough to cancel the epidural injection within a couple of weeks. And as of this writing, I have not had any further back issues. Praise God.

## PERFECT DONOR FOR MJ

*Hope is not a granted wish or a favor performed; no, it is far greater than that. It is a zany, unpredictable dependence on a God who loves to surprise us out of our socks.*

—MAX LUCADO (LUCADO AND HALL 2021)

Just after Labor Day, MJ and I received calls that a donor match was available for her. The national registry was working out the details, and we would hear soon about surgery dates. We were both excited after waiting nearly five months. MJ would finally be free from dialysis.

But then, several days later, we received a call saying the donation chain collapsed. We were both initially disappointed, but we reminded ourselves it wasn't a perfect match. We continued to pray.

Our BSF class began a new study on September 12, 2016. My new role as the class teaching leader started. During our opening session, I introduced Bill. Then, I asked our discussion groups, the entire class, to pray for the *perfect* kidney match for MJ.

Several weeks later. In early October, MJ and I got phone calls from our respective transplant coordinators. A *perfect* match for MJ became available. We learned a young man in his twenties walked into a hospital in South Carolina and said he wanted to donate his kidney to anyone who needed one.

According to the matching criteria for kidney transplantation, I was rated a three out of five for MJ. However, this young man was a five out of five. He was her *perfect* match. Prayer answered!

But God had bigger plans. He answered the prayers of sixteen recipients simultaneously, all because one young man offered to donate his kidney to anyone who needed one. His selfless gift triggered a chain of matches through the Paired Exchange national registry.

After more than a year from when we first started praying for MJ and almost six months from when we became an eligible matched pair, MJ and my surgeries would take place. My surgery took place at 7 a.m. A team was waiting to bring my kidney to Richmond airport for a trip to San Francisco. Shortly after, the young man in South Carolina had his surgery, and a private plane transported his kidney to Richmond. MJ was prepped and ready by late morning to receive her *"perfect"* kidney.

The logistics were mind-numbing. Over the next ten to fourteen days, thirty-two surgeries would occur nationwide. Sixteen recipients experienced the miracle of new life. But God wasn't done with miracles.

After surgery, they wanted me and MJ up and moving quickly. Our respective nurses advised us to take pain medicine to avoid discomfort while walking. We both agreed, and that was the only time we had pain medication post-surgery! But God still wasn't done. He had one more miracle.

Before surgery, the transplant surgeon told MJ it typically takes a few days for a new kidney to work correctly. However, after her surgery, the doctor told MJ the new kidney began to function and process urine immediately after it was transplanted. He told her he couldn't recall that happening in all his surgeries.

Only God can do what is humanly impossible. In His timing, the *perfect* match became available. Hundreds of people who had been praying for MJ experienced an answered prayer.

 As of this writing, MJ is doing fabulously. Because her match was perfect, she only required the lowest dose of anti-rejection medicine, which reduced her overall health risks from the medication's side effects.

When I was preparing to write this chapter, Bill, MJ, and I had a Zoom call. We all agreed the journey was remarkable. We are still amazed at how God ordered steps, timing, and people in a way no one could have planned or orchestrated.

MJ shared a conversation she had with her medical doctor. He told her he had never had a patient who went into kidney failure that quickly. MJ told the doctor confidently, "I think that was part of God's plan. If my kidneys had failed slowly, I would have been too old to have a transplant."

### REFLECTIONS

I hope this story will inspire you to consider being a living donor. You can make a difference for one person. And you will write a new chapter in your story.

Let me challenge all of us with Andy's words: "Do for one what you wish you could do for everyone" (Stanley 2019).

If you would like further information, visit the websites of the National Kidney Foundation, Donate Life, and the American Liver Foundation.

Your generous gift will offer hope to someone in need and give them a better quality of life.

CHAPTER 18

# WALKING BRINGS HOPE

*You are someone else's miracle! God is setting up divine
appointments and it is our job to keep them*

—MARK BATTERSON

## WALKING INTO SPIRITUAL HEALTH

As I've mentioned throughout this book, I enjoy walking outdoors. I've been doing it for years. When I traveled on business,
walking was like an expedition as I explored new cities by
taking in the sights and sounds. It's also a great way to connect with my thoughts. In addition, I listen to audiobooks or
podcasts and pray. The extra benefit is that it's great exercise.

Living in Florida, I could walk all year round, something I
couldn't do in New Jersey because the winters were too cold.
My walking buddy was Reese, my son's dog. Our home was in
Lake Mary, and the Cross Seminole Trail began right outside
the entrance to our community, Silver Lake.

We would start at the trailhead and travel north toward
Lake Mary Boulevard. Reese and I started early morning during
the coolest part of the day. We had plenty of company, with

folks walking, biking, or rollerblading. We often met our neighbors who were also out for a walk.

People we didn't know would soon become walking companions, with whom we shared some great conversations and memories.

I saw an older white-haired gentleman with a long, white beard walking with his head down, apparently deep in thought. As I passed him, I offered an enthusiastic greeting, "Good morning. Enjoy your walk," or "Have a great day."

This guy never responded—not even a head nod. Instead, he kept his head down. What little of his face I could see revealed someone in deep thought and troubled. This pattern continued for months.

One morning months later, I passed him after my typical smile and greeting. Within seconds, I heard from behind me, "Hello! Excuse me." As I turned around, he was walking toward me. For the first time, I saw his entire face, head up.

He said, "You have a peace about you that I don't have. I want peace. How do I get it?

After all these months, this older gentleman and I were engaged in conversation while walking. He was more animated and energetic. He told me his name. I struggled to pronounce his first name, so I called him Mr. Gorham. He was born in India. His parents were diplomats stationed in Ethiopia who eventually moved to England, where he attended university. Later his family settled in Canada, where he maintained a residence. After retiring, he spent many months at a time in Lake Mary with his daughter and her family. We spoke like long-lost friends catching up.

We eventually got back to his original question about obtaining peace. I told Mr. Gorham my niece, Jennifer, had been abducted, which brought me to my knees in grief. I was brutally honest about my life and how things began to change after I accepted Jesus.

Mr. Gorham, with an inquisitive look, asked, "What do you mean? How did Jesus change your life?"

As a newbie Christian, my mind froze momentarily, trying to think of something to say. "Well, that's going to take some time to explain." I shared that Debbie and I were attending a new church and learning a lot from the pastors' messages and that I enjoyed reading my Bible.

Mr. Gorham looked at me and sympathetically said, "My condolences to you and your family. I'm sorry to hear you had to go through that much pain."

Thankful to have a few seconds to think, I said, "A guy I used to work with invited me to a Bible study group, which I am still attending. I'm learning a lot, and that's why I enjoy reading it."

Mr. Gorham had his head down again and got quiet. He appeared to be processing our conversation. The rest of our walk was silent. As we approached the trail's end, I told him how much I enjoyed talking with him and looked forward to another day. He nodded his head in agreement.

The next time I saw Mr. Gorham, he smiled and allowed me to walk with him. Over time as we became comfortable with each other, our discussions became more intense. Finally, one day, Mr. Gorham blurted out, "I'm Hindu, so I don't understand Christianity's focus on one person. Hinduism has many different traditions and philosophies."

*That came out of nowhere.* "That sounds pretty complicated," I replied, "In Christianity, it's all about Jesus, which makes it easier to think about."

Mr. Gorham told me many paths exist to reaching the god you are worshipping in Hinduism. As he was talking, I could tell by his body language and tone of voice he was frustrated trying to grapple with all the different ideas about God. Yet, from our discussions, he was curious and seeking answers and understanding.

He then said something puzzling. "I am interested in learning about other religions from someone practicing it."

*He doesn't practice what he shared about Hinduism. Now I know why he asks so many questions.* "What do you mean?" I asked him.

Mr. Gorham answered, "Well, you've told me you're going to church and studying your Bible, right? That means you're practicing your religion. I'm not involved in any religion. But I want to hear about yours."

Over the next several days, we walked and talked about God and religion in general terms. Then, one morning, our conversation got interesting. Mr. Gorham pivoted the conversation abruptly and said, "What do you think happens when you die?"

Before I could respond, he said, "Hindus believe in reincarnation and karma that results in a cycle of rebirths, and the goal is to work on improving your behavior so that cycle stops."

"Did I hear you right? The goal is to work on improving your behavior?" I responded. At the time, I barely understood the Christian faith and had only heard about the concept of reincarnation.

"From what you told me, that has to be exhausting and frustrating—trying to work on being better. How do you know if you've done enough? Is there a standard?" I continued, looking over at him as he nodded in agreement.

"You don't," Mr. Gorham replied in a sad tone.

That conversation reminded me of one of the reasons I had stopped going to church as a teenager. Religions have a lot of rules. One thing we generally dislike is rules. Our instinct is to push back on them. We also like looking for loopholes to avoid doing anything we don't like. *I'm smiling. If I can't find a loophole, I'll devise a rationalization that allows me to do what I want.* Crazy!

I believe Mr. Gorham and I touched on something without realizing it. Our performance. It determines rewards, benefits, or some form of criticism and punishment. Win, lose; pass, fail. When we're good, we get a reward. If we're bad, we get punished. If we perform well in school, we'll get a good job. If we perform well at work, we get a promotion. We understand performance matters in many aspects of life. However, I have learned from experience it gets in the way of understanding what matters most to God. Why? Because universally, we believe He looks at our performance.

Think about the questions we ask. What must I do to get on God's good side? How good do I have to be to get into heaven? What's the standard? Is there a checklist I can follow?

Thankfully, God has made it clear He does not look at our performance, status, money, job title, or any of what we believe are "good" works.

In a moment of clarity, I shared with Mr. Gorham, "I don't fully understand my faith yet. I'm still learning. But one thing I know for sure: the God I'm learning about did not leave my present or future to chance. And it has nothing to do with my behavior or performance. I don't have to do anything to get right with God."

He looked at me incredulously. "What do you mean you don't have to do anything?"

*This is going to get interesting.* My mind was searching for the right words. I said, "Remember when I told you about Jennifer?" He nodded his head. "I was a mess. I had lunch with a former coworker who knew my situation, and he asked me if I wanted to invite God into my life, so I did. That's when I started reading the Bible. I didn't do anything different. I wasn't 'working' on my behavior. I was just learning about God. And I now have peace that I didn't have before."

> *Jesus didn't come to tell us the answers to the questions of life; he came to be the answer.*
> —TIMOTHY KELLER (KELLER 2017)

Our time together ended, so this conversation just hung in the air as we said goodbye.

A few days later, I walked behind Mr. Gorham and shouted, "Good morning!"

He turned and looked at me with a big smile and excitedly said, "I want to get a copy of a Bible!"

I was so enthusiastic he was interested that I immediately started explaining the different versions and language styles. But he interrupted me.

"No, I want to know the name of the original Bible."

I took a moment to think. "I think you're talking about the King James Version."

Mr. Gorham replied, "That's it; that's the one I'm going to get."

The next time I saw him on the trail, he couldn't wait to tell me that he got his King James Bible and was reading it. He was smiling and excited. What a difference from all those months ago when he wouldn't even look at me. I could tell his mind was swirling. Based on our conversations, what he was now reading made more sense than what challenged him about Hinduism.

He saw my big smile and smiled back. I was excited for him. Mr. Gorham was experiencing a peace that had eluded him for years. He realized his eternal certainty was not tied to trying to satisfy multiple lowercase-G gods, but to the God of the Bible.

One morning months later, we met on the trail. Mr. Gorham eagerly told me he had connected with an old friend and shared with him what was happening in his life and his new hope. So, in another divine appointment, that friend, after several conversations, prayed with him as he accepted Jesus as his Savior and Lord. He now had certain hope.

*Anything of spiritual significance that happens in your life will be a result of God's activity in you. He is infinitely more concerned with your life and your relationship with Him than you or I could possibly be.*

—HENRY T. BLACKABY (BLACKABY ET AL. 2008)

Wow! Only God can orchestrate what started as two people walking past each other daily to a transformed life.

Even with my little knowledge and understanding, God planned a divine appointment at the right time, and "that man" on the trail was ready to talk.

Some may wonder why I would have continued to greet someone who had ignored me for so long. My answer is simple: I ignored God for nearly fifty years, and He never gave up on me. Besides, it's easy to smile and greet people. It's part of who I am. However, I would have stopped saying anything if you had ignored me before January 2006.

Without us being aware, God is working with someone right now. It could be you. It might be someone you know. Either way, being prepared would be a wise decision.

## HOW A CAR OPENED A CONVERSATION

*Since God knows our future, our personalities, and*
*our capacity to listen, He isn't ever going to say*
*more to us than we can deal with at the moment.*

—DR. CHARLES F. STANLEY (STANLEY 2002)

More than a year after meeting Mr. Gorham in the early mornings, my work schedule changed, so Reese and I took our
walks later in the morning. The downside is it's much hotter
and more humid as the day progresses. The upside: we'd meet
different folks on the trail.

One of those was a fellow who wore the Publix "uniform": black pants and a green polo shirt with the company
logo. Another opportunity to warmly greet someone, which
I did, but this time, the response was always a smile, and he
returned the greeting.

One late morning I had been out for an appointment,
and I saw my "Publix" friend walking south on Longwood
Lake Mary Road toward the city of Longwood. It was hot
and humid. He was far from the Cross Seminole Trail. I got
a nudge to turn around and talk to him, so I did. Pulling
up near him, I rolled the passenger window down and said
hello. As soon as he recognized me, he smiled and came
to the car.

We acknowledged seeing each other on the trail. I asked,
"Where are you walking to?"

He said, "To my part-time job."

I followed up, "Where?"

He says, "Burger King."

Surprised and in disbelief, I said, "Burger King? The one
on 17/92?"

He replied, "Yes."

I quickly responded, "That's at least three miles from here."

He nodded his head in agreement.

I responded, "Come on, get into the car. I'll take you to work."

During the drive, we introduced ourselves. His name was Nader, and he lived in a neighborhood close to our home. I learned he had part-time jobs at Publix and Burger King. He had been walking to both jobs for quite a while. He told me his family only had one car, which his wife drove. She worked much farther from home, so he walked to his workplace.

I then asked, "Do you have a ride home? I'd be happy to come and get you."

Nader said, "Thank you, but my wife will pick me up on her way home."

Arriving at his work, he thanked me profusely, repeatedly shaking my hand with a huge smile.

The next time I saw Nader, he was on the trail walking to Publix. This time I didn't pass him by. I walked at his pace up to the intersection of the Publix shopping center. This allowed us to get to know each other.

Nader immigrated to the United States from Iran and had been a mechanical engineer in his home country. He also served in the Iranian Army. When he arrived in this country, he was older. Struggling to learn English created academic obstacles. As a result, he couldn't get an engineering license in the United States. Instead, he and his wife worked multiple jobs to support their family.

I enjoyed spending time with Nader. He was always upbeat with a positive attitude despite the challenges he had faced. However, at times he was reserved, even a bit guarded. At the time, I told Nader that I worked from home and was happy to drive him to either job whenever I was in town. I gave him my cell phone number, and he gave me his home number.

Several times our paths crossed while walking. Though he never called to take me up on the offer to take him to work, if I was driving and saw him walking, I'd stop, pick him up, and take him to work.

Our son Nick, who was in the army, was home for Christmas break in 2008, and one day we were out on an errand. I saw Nader wearing his Burger King uniform shirt. We turned around and picked him up. I introduced Nick to Nader, and they shared army stories during the drive.

I interrupted their conversation, "Nader. Nick is returning to his base next week. We planned on donating this van [a 1999 Plymouth Voyager] to a local charity. I would like you to have it."

Nader looked at me in disbelief. "No, no, I can't accept this van," he pushed back.

"I said, why not? Wouldn't a second car be helpful?" Before he could say anything, I continued. "We really are going to donate this van, so please take it."

With a big smile, Nader said, "If you are going to donate it, I'll take it. But are you sure?"

"Yes, I'll reach out to you after Nick leaves and we'll coordinate going to the DMV office to transfer the van."

The following week, we made the arrangements and transferred the van to Nader.

This story took a humorous turn. One day Debbie was out running errands and saw Nader walking to work. She called me and asked, "Did something happen to the van? I just saw Nader walking to work."

"I have no idea, but I'll find out the next time I see him," I replied.

A couple of days later, I see Nader walking on the trail. "Nader, is everything okay with the van? Debbie said she saw you walking to work the other day?"

Nader smiled, almost laughing, "Everything is fine with the van. But I've put on some weight from not walking as much, so I decided to start walking more."

We both laughed, as did Debbie when I told her.

Nader then asked what I thought was an odd question considering we had gotten to know each other. "Why did you give the van to me? You didn't really know me."

I immediately realized this was a divine appointment. I told Nader, "My niece Jennifer was abducted in January 2006, and my life changed as a result."

Before I could continue, Nader interrupted, "Jennifer... your niece is Jennifer Kesse. I remember that story; it's been in the news for a couple of years. I'm so sorry. I didn't know she was your niece."

I continued. "Yes, and no worries. It's not like it would have come up in conversation. But Jenn's abduction caused me to be more aware of the needs of other people, and whenever I can, I want to help. You needed an extra vehicle, and we were getting rid of the van, so it worked out for both of us."

That conversation changed our relationship from that moment on. After that, if we walked on the trail together, we talked about our families and learned about our backgrounds. We discussed the uncertainties of life, religion, and God.

One day Nader said, "I was raised as a Muslim and in Islam, and I have no certainty about my eternal fate because it is in the hands of Allah."

I asked him to explain a bit more, and he shared, "As a Muslim, I was taught that my destiny is whatever Allah has determined for me. I try to do all I can to be good, to treat others well, that my intentions are good, but in the end, I will die and not know whether I've done enough good things to overcome any bad".

My heart sank. Nader, "I'm so sorry; I can't even imagine the weight of uncertainty you carry."

I shared my story of accepting Jesus into my life and what He has been doing in me. I was learning by attending First Baptist Orlando and going to bible study. Nader told me he wanted to know more, and we agreed to carry that conversation for another day.

I went to Books-A-Million, bought Nader *The Every Man's Bible*, and gave it to him as a gift. I suggested he begin reading Matthew and John first, which would give us something to discuss.

Nader began reading the Bible, and we had some great discussions. It was encouraging to see Nader's eagerness to learn and understand the Bible. I invited him to join our Bible study group, but Mondays didn't work due to work commitments.

One afternoon, I saw Nader working at Publix. He walked over to me with a big smile and said, "Bill, I've started going to Northland [a nondenominational church in Longwood, Florida]." He told me he enjoyed Pastor Joel Hunter's teaching and the music.

All I could think to say was, "Wow! That's terrific. I am happy for you and your family."

A few weeks later, we saw each other, and he told me he would be baptized and that he had accepted Jesus as His Savior. I immediately hugged him, congratulated him, and told him I'd like to be there for him. But unfortunately, I would be out of state on business on the day of his baptism. I was disappointed not to be with him but so excited God was working in his life.

A few days before his baptism, I went to Publix. Walking into the store, I saw Nader at a table outside. His head was down, looking like the world's weight was on his shoulders. I sat next to him and asked, "Nader, what's going on? You look like you lost your best friend."

Nader said softly and without his characteristic smile, "I am feeling guilty, fearful, and anxious."

I asked him, "Why?"

"My mind filled with thoughts about abandoning my Muslim faith. I'm worried about how this will impact my family if I get baptized. I love going to Northland. I'm learning a lot. In my heart, I know this is the right decision. But now I'm torn."

Nader was clearly wrestling over a significant change in his life.

I paused for a moment and asked God for the right words to offer him. I placed my hand on his knee, looked into his eyes, and said, "Nader, instead of thinking you're walking away from something or abandoning your childhood faith, I believe that over the past months, God is helping you see things from a new perspective. His. You're not abandoning your faith; you're moving in a new direction. Your faith will be strengthened, and you will be a good role model for your family."

Nader's countenance brightened. He looked at me and said, "Do you really believe that?"

"Yes, I'm positive." I continued, "I've watched how God has given you the desire to know Him. You are excited to learn. Remember when I told you that the closer you move toward God, the more resistance you will experience? That's what's happening right now. Be encouraged; God is with you. Lean in and remain firm in your decision and pray. I'll be praying for you."

The Nader I knew and loved was back—with a big smile, thanking me with repeated handshaking and a bounce in his step. He returned to work, and he got baptized.

 When I travel to Florida, I always try to visit Nader and check in on him and his family. They are all doing well, and we always greet each other with a smile and a bear hug.

*When we obey God, we will experience His blessings;*
*when we don't, we will miss out on that blessing.*
*One of the most basic yet important principles a*
*Christian can ever learn is that of obedience.*
— DR. CHARLES F. STANLEY (STANLEY 2005, 85)

## REFLECTIONS

I've shared just two of the many encounters I've had the privilege of having with people. Whether by chance or design, I left those conversations more encouraged and alive.

Every day I think about Jennifer. I am wondering, waiting for answers. One thing I know for sure is God works in our pain and suffering. If we invite Him into our lives, He will show us how our experiences can help others. It remains a mystery to me. Yet, in meeting Mr. Gorham and Nader, my vulnerability opened the doors to hearts that had been closed or partially open.

I did not plan to meet these men, but I was prepared to engage in meaningful conversations, even with little knowledge. All I needed to do was be willing and available to talk about what God had done in me. It was easy to share what I had experienced. After all, it's my story. No one can argue with me about it.

Importantly, I didn't feel the need to start quoting Bible verses. I couldn't anyway because I only had a few verses memorized that were meaningful to me. As Bill Rush had done for me, I acted like a highway offramp sign and pointed Nader and Mr. Gorham to the only person who could help them, Jesus. Over the years, I've seen many people make sharing their personal stories more complicated than they need to be. It's straightforward. Just share with enthusiasm what God has done for you. He'll do the rest. He just wants us to be available and ready to share.

Rick Warren, pastor and author of *The Purpose Driven Life*, wrote,

*Shared stories build a relational bridge that Jesus can walk across from your heart to others* (WARREN 2012, 288).

Are you ready to share your story? If not, take some time to write it out, and then organize it so you can remember the highlights to bring out in conversations. One of my regular prayers is, "Lord, put someone in my path who needs to know you today, open my heart to recognize them, and be ready to walk with them."

PART SIX

# CALL TO ACTION

# CHAPTER 19

# SEEKING IDENTITY AND PURPOSE

*It is only in God that we discover our origin, our identity, our meaning, our purpose, our significance, and our destiny. Every other path leads to a dead end.*

—RICK WARREN

From my first job at fourteen until I approached my fiftieth birthday, I sought identity, purpose, and meaning in my life through work and the commitment to serve in many community organizations. Serving is an excellent thing to do. It feels great to be doing something worthwhile and simultaneously helping others. Yet that feeling is fleeting.

Busyness is like that. We keep busy filling the holes in our lives, only to realize we are leaking out the things we seek. The cycle repeats. We strive to maintain our source of identity, purpose, and meaning, which requires us to increase earning, learning, and winning at all costs.

Looking back on my life, it is clear where I *was* seeking identity. But from where or whom *should* I have sought identity?

One book helped me get out of the ditch and back on the right road—the road to understanding myself, my life's meaning, and my purpose: the Bible.

Despite 2006 beginning tragically, 2007 began with renewed energy and enthusiasm. Having found my identity in Jesus Christ, I no longer needed to work at or strive to find meaning. I was no longer exhausted from depending on myself.

Read Paul's words to followers of Jesus in Ephesus: "It's in Christ that we find out who we are and what we are living for. Long before we first heard of Christ and got our hopes up, he had his eye on us, had designs on us for glorious living, part of the overall purpose he is working out in everything and everyone" (Ephesians 1:11-12, MSG).

Tired and exhausted from striving and working hard to please yourself and others? Jesus' invitation two thousand years ago is still valid today:

*Come to me, all you who are weary and burdened, and I will give you rest. Take my yoke on you and learn from me, because I am gentle and humble in heart, and you will find rest for your souls.*
—JESUS OF NAZARETH (MATTHEW 11:28-29, NET)

---

**CALL TO ACTION**

Do you remember my stories about nudges and stirrings? If you just felt a prompt, please stop reading and immediately accept Jesus' invitation out loud if you would like. You'll feel relieved and ready for your next step. I was!

## THE PURPOSE-DRIVEN LIFE

My first step in January 2007 was to read Rick Warren's *The Purpose Driven Life: What on Earth Am I Here For?* The book is designed to be read one chapter a day for forty days, and that is what I did. The timing was perfect. With five months of Bible study under my belt, I wanted to focus on my life's purpose.

Beginning on page nine, *A Journey with a Purpose: Getting the Most from This Book* reinforced the timing was perfect; I'm on a quest for understanding. I was encouraged to read: "The best way to explain God's purpose for your life is to allow the Scripture to speak for itself, so in this book the Bible is quoted extensively, using over a thousand different verses from fifteen English translations and paraphrases" (Warren 2002, 11).

I opened the book to the content page and read the first section heading, "What on Earth Am I Here For?" That is a great question. I wanted to know the answer. In this section, we covered:

> *It all starts with God.*
> *You are not an accident.*
> *Seeing life from God's view* (WARREN 2002, CONTENTS).

In purpose one, "You Were Planned for God's Pleasure," two ideas caught my attention:

> *Becoming Best Friends with God.*
> *When God Seems Distant* (WARREN 2002, CONTENTS).

I knew this would be a great investment of time, and I was not disappointed. Every one of us has looked up into a clear dark sky, amazed by the brilliance of the stars, and contemplated the vastness of space. While looking into that night sky, we asked questions. Why are we here? Why now? What's our purpose? Where do we fit in?

Scientific advances have provided the ability for you and me to "see" and know the truth about God and creation.

The psalmist wrote, "The heavens declare the glory of God, and the sky above proclaims his handiwork" (Psalm 19:1, ESV).

The apostle Paul wrote, "What can be known about God is plain to them, because God has made it plain to them. For since the creation of the world, his invisible attributes—his eternal power and divine nature—have been clearly seen, because they are understood through what has been made. So people are without excuse" (Romans 1:19-20, NET).

Robert Roberson wrote a book with a great title: *The Bible Is Our Basic Instructions Before Leaving Earth.* For centuries, theologians and followers of Jesus believed God inspired the authors to write the words in the Bible, basic instructions for mankind to know how to live with each other and rightly with God.

---

**CALL TO ACTION**

No more excuses. If you want to learn God's basic instructions for a purposeful life, start reading the Bible. For the best results, get involved in an in-depth Bible study. I highly recommend Bible Study Fellowship (bsfinternational.org).

---

Back to *The Purpose Driven Life.* Day one, *It All Starts with God: It's not about you. The purpose of your life is far greater than your own personal fulfillment, your peace of mind, or even your happiness. It's far greater than your family, your career, or even your wildest dreams and ambitions. If you want to know why you are placed on this planet, you must begin with God. You were born by his purpose and for his purpose* (WARREN 2012, 21).

Rick mentioned something that resonated with me. If we want to know how something works, we need the owner's manual. More times than I can count or recall, I only looked at the owner's manual or operating instructions *after* trying to figure it out on my own. I remember all those Christmas presents with "some assembly required" that I attempted to put together without reading the instructions. *I'll figure it out.* Wrong!

As it turns out, I was wrong about trying to "assemble" my life. Thankfully, I'm doing a better job *listening* now. Sometimes.

One of the important basic instructions we need to know and apply is "don't copy the behavior and customs of this world, but let God transform you into a new person by changing the way you think. Then you will learn to know God's will for you, which is good and pleasing and perfect" (Romans 12:2, NLT).

Wise advice. It would have been helpful beginning in my teenage years.

On day two, I learned I wasn't an accident. My birth date, city, and parents were planned by God. The chapter verse was "I am your Creator. You were in my care even before you were born" (Isaiah 44:2a, CEV).

Up until this point, it never occurred to me that I was planned for a purpose, instead of being some random, unexpected event. Wow! The idea that God knows every detail of me, physically, emotionally, and spiritually, was unnerving—especially since I didn't know myself that well. When King

David had his epiphany on this important issue, he wrote these insightful words:

*O Lord, you have examined my heart and know everything about me. You made all the delicate, inner parts of my body and knit me together in my mother's womb. You watched me as I was being formed in utter seclusion, as I was woven together in the dark of the womb. You saw me before I was born. Every day of my life was recorded in your book. Every moment was laid out before a single day had passed.* (PSALM 139: 1,13,15–16, NLT)

On day five, *Seeing Life from God's View:* we learned that the way you and I see ourselves, our lives, and how we process the words spoken into our lives shape the person we become.

Rick wrote, "The Bible offers three metaphors that teach us God's view of life: Life is a *test*, life is a *trust*, and life is a *temporary assignment*. These ideas are the foundation of purpose-driven living" (Warren 2002, 42).

Throughout the biblical narrative, we see many individuals or nations who experienced times of testing, trials, temptations, and refining. According to *The Purpose Driven Life*, those words occur over two hundred times. Beginning with Adam and Eve, we read about well-known people such as Noah, Job, Abraham, Joseph, David, and Esther, to name a few, who experienced some form of testing, trials, temptations, or refining.

As I thought about this concept, I realized this had been a consistent part of my life in some form or another. Without realizing it, my character was being developed *and* observed. How did I respond to the challenges? Often poorly. It had never occurred to me that my life has been a test, and those trials and tests continue. King David brought home the idea of how much God knows about us.

> *You know when I sit down or stand up. You know my thoughts even when I'm far away. You see me when I travel and when I rest at home. You know everything I do. You know what I am going to say even before I say it, Lord. You go before me and follow me. I can never escape from your Spirit! I can never get away from your presence!* (PSALM 139:2–5,7, NLT)

The idea that God *knows* everything about me was very sobering. Maybe a bit frightening. So much remains hidden in the recesses of my thoughts, but not from God. This was a serious wake-up call.

---

**CALL TO ACTION**
If God has called something to your mind–a habit or lifestyle choice that needs to change, or maybe it's seeking or offering forgiveness to someone; whatever it is, stop reading, seek God, and do whatever He asks you to do.

---

On day eleven, "becoming best friends with God" was a concept I'd never heard of before nor considered possible. At first, I thought, *What? How can this be? He is up there in heaven, and I'm down here on earth.*

Something Rick said brought back childhood memories of my bad church experiences. "Moses and Abraham were called 'friends of God,' David was called a man after [God's] own heart, and Job, Enoch, and Noah had intimate relationships with God. But fear of God, not friendship, was more common in the Old Testament" (Warren 2002, 85–86).

This shouldn't have been surprising. In the first book of the Bible, Genesis, we read that God walked and talked with Adam and Eve. They were in a relationship with God.

I challenged myself to thoughtfully consider the question at the end of day eleven: "What can I do to remind myself to think about God and talk to him more often throughout the day?" (Warren 2002, 91).

My thinking was challenged. I sensed a prompting to pay attention to this question—to be intentional about prioritizing God in every part of my day. No easy task. My first decision: get up early every day and spend time with God by reading the Bible, talking, listening, and praying.

---

**CALL TO ACTION**

What does your calendar or checkbook reveal about what is most important to you? Maybe it's time to evaluate your priorities and reorganize your day so you can put God first.

---

When I got to day fourteen, "When God Seems Distant," I was reminded Jennifer was still missing. We had no answers as to what had happened. My relationship with God was new, and I felt encouraged. However, my prayers remained unanswered. Doubt began to creep into my thinking. I read, "The most common mistake Christians make...is seeking an experience rather than seeking God." Rick then wrote:

*When you are a baby Christian (which I was at the time), God gives you a lot of confirming emotions and often answers the most immature, self-centered prayers (which he did)—so you'll know he exists. But as you grow in faith, he will wean you off these dependencies* (WARREN 2002, 109).

The light bulb went on in my mind. Focus on what I know is true, what God has said. King David shared his insights—God knows every intricate detail of our lives. I can't hide from Him. The wise choice is to get real and raw with Him about anything and everything I'm feeling and experiencing. He knows my heart. Most importantly, He is the solution.

One beautiful Florida morning, while working in my home office, I became frustrated by the lack of progress on Jennifer's case. *I'm really pissed off, God. I'm trying my best to understand You and everything I'm learning. Why haven't You answered my prayers?* I sat there, and at that moment, I screamed out loud at God. I verbally dumped my pent-up frustrations and the "why" questions.

Physically and emotionally exhausted from screaming, I lay flat on the floor and got quiet. I briefly fell asleep. When I woke up, I felt refreshed, calm, and at peace. I didn't have clarity about what I had just yelled about. But getting it out felt good. Besides, God already knew.

I remembered times with my children when they were at a breaking point. Debbie and I encouraged them to let it out so they would feel better. At that moment, I imagined God, my heavenly Father, smiling and saying, "Do you feel better? I've got this. Don't worry."

The reality was beginning to set in. I was part of a new family: God's. An important community of people who experience life together and are there to help each other.

My forty-day reading of *The Purpose Driven Life* concluded with a challenge. Rick mentioned that in the Book of Acts, Luke wrote, "David...served the purpose of God in his own generation." God described David as "a man after my heart, who will do my will" (Acts 13:22, 36, ESV).

You and I were designed and expected to serve God. To do that, we need to be prepared and understand our unique gifts, talents, and skills, and then use them for the benefit of other people.

I have been honored to serve God in several capacities, which have been discussed in earlier chapters. But I believe my highest service has been writing this book. During my early prayer and preparation, He was clear: I would share vulnerably and authentically. Everything was known by God and me. Some things were known by others. However, I've hung it all out there with the hope and prayer that you will experience God for the first time or in a new way. My goal was to inspire hope so life transformation would take place.

CHAPTER 20

# SEVENTEEN YEARS LATER

*"We want to thank the public who continues to support our efforts to find our daughter, Jennifer. You have never given up, and we truly feel that from you. The job is not done, so please – if you know something, say something! One day it might be you or your loved ones looking for the public's help. We know that together we can bring Jennifer's pain to an end.*

*Jennifer, we love you and miss you tremendously. We will not give up, we will not shut up, and we will do everything possible to bring you home."*

—JOYCE AND DREW KESSE

We end our time together with the question I asked at the end of Chapter 1 — How does someone vanish without a trace? We know someone has information about what happened to Jenn and can identify the person of interest from the surveillance video. Why are they unwilling to come forward?

Unfortunately, as we have discussed, for many people, it's all about *self*. As hard as it is to read or hear, self-preservation, self-denial, and plain selfishness drive behaviors that result in emotional, relational, and physical pain.

This reality of *self* has had a lasting impact on my family, especially Joyce, Drew, Jennifer, and Logan. After Drew read the sentence above, he said, "That sums up what we've been dealing with the past seventeen years perfectly." Sadly, why is that a true statement that our family and yours must experience?

## THE PROBLEM WITH PEOPLE

Over the past chapters, we talked about a variety of universal issues. Our tendency to be self-focused creates obstacles as we try to seek meaning and purpose in our lives while living rightly with other people. The tension is palpable and undeniable. The challenge is whether we are willing to face the truth about ourselves. Are we willing to stop lying to ourselves and others? Will we open our hearts and be vulnerable? Will we pursue life transformation?

We explored the importance of listening, the challenges we face in learning how to listen actively and reflectively, as well as speaking the truth, being honest, and acting with integrity.

Our words, actions, and inaction matter. They can encourage and inspire, or they can discourage and demoralize. The impact of our words and lack of action creates an incalculable ripple effect. And while these are all words on this page — they are intensely personal to our family.

Everyone loses when our words and actions are not encouraging or helpful.

This is the essence of the despair and heartbreak that Joyce and Drew have endured over the past seventeen years. Why?

The answer is that many of the people they have interacted with failed to demonstrate basic human decency and compassion. They choose not to place themselves in my sister and brother-in-law's shoes. They failed to ask themselves a simple question — if this was *my* daughter or family member, how would I want *their* case handled?

## JENNIFER IS STILL MISSING, DO THE RIGHT THING

In Chapter 11, we discussed the TV show *What Would You Do?* Unsuspecting people were placed in situations that created raw emotional responses – how will they respond – what will they do?

While *What Would You Do?* is a "reality" show, our family is still living the reality of the raw emotions from that Tuesday seventeen years ago. But *that* question still needs to be answered by the people directly or indirectly involved in Jenn's case, or by anyone who has information that will help bring her home or bring closure to her case.

As we have discussed, it's never too late to change. We can choose to make things right. Doing the right things never has an expiration date. We may start our lives or careers poorly, but we can choose to finish well. One day every individual *will* be personally held accountable for every word, thought, and action.

What do you want people to say about you when you are gone? Are you prepared to do the right things now so that your story and legacy finish well?

**CALL TO ACTION**

**After seventeen long years, our family is thankful that on November 28, 2022, Jennifer's case was transferred to the Florida Department of Law Enforcement (FDLE) for a cold case review. We look forward to the FDLE doing the following:**

- Meeting with the family's investigative team.
- Speaking to the individuals identified by their investigative team.
- Resubmitting all physical evidence for forensic review.
- Reviewing all case files and findings.
- Speaking with specific individuals who have been identified during the investigation.

*"If, after all these items have been completed, and there is no clear path to solving Jennifer's case, we can finally rest. We will know that we did everything we could do to seek answers."*

—JOYCE & DREW KESSE

**CALL TO ACTION**

**Help Us Find Jennifer**

We would greatly appreciate your help. To stay informed about her case, please visit **Help Us Find Jennifer** on the **GoFundMe** website.

## CALL TO ACTION

**PRAYER REQUESTS**

Only God and the people involved in Jenn's abduction know where she is and what happened. We would appreciate your prayers, specifically for the following:

Pray for God to provide wisdom, insight, and discernment to the FDLE staff and any other individuals as they work to reconstruct Jenn's case from the beginning to the present.

As the FDLE begins interviews, pray that God breaks the hearts of anyone directly or indirectly involved or with knowledge of what happened to Jennifer so they will come forward and speak truthfully.

Pray for courage for Chino, who is believed to have information about Jenn's case, so he will come forward and cooperate.

Dr. Martin Luther King, Jr. said in his Nobel Peace Prize acceptance speech in 1964:
*"I believe that unarmed truth and unconditional love will have the final word in reality. This is why right, temporarily defeated, is stronger than evil triumphant"* (KING, JR.).

## FINAL CALL TO ACTION

### INVITATION

**The bottom line:** Just take your first step toward knowing and experiencing God. Over time you and the people in your life will become eyewitnesses to God's truths as you become more loving, joyful, patient, kind, and generous. You are the best evidence that life change is possible as the people in your life see those character qualities in action – consistently exercising self-control and patience.

### ONE DECISION AWAY

If you believe Jesus is the Son of God and that He died for you, then tell Him you believe. Ask Him to forgive your sins and invite Him into your life and then follow Him. He is waiting on you and can't wait to start working with you.

### THANK YOU!

To every reader, thank you! Thank you for choosing to buy this book and following along with me as I shared my quest for understanding that led to life transformation. I hope that the personal stories you've read have offered inspiring life lessons that will make a difference in your life.

If at any point while you were reading, you felt that nudge or prompt, I hope you said *yes* to God's invitation to begin your journey to becoming a better *you*. If you did — Congratulations!

**I would love to hear from you. Contact me by visiting www.inspiringhopedaily.com. You will also find additional resources to help you with your next steps.**

# ACKNOWLEDGMENTS

*No one who achieves success does so without
acknowledging the help of others. The wise and
confident acknowledge this help with gratitude.*
—ALFRED NORTH WHITEHEAD

After drifting through the uncertain waters of life for nearly fifty years, God reached out, grabbed my hand, and pulled me into His boat. I am eternally grateful You never gave up on me! Thank you for providing and preparing the way to get this book completed through Kaity Van Riper, a talented and creative writer and editor who happens to be the daughter of Peggy and Brian Krompasick, our friends for over forty-two years. Kaity enthusiastically introduced me to New Degree Press and Professor Eric Koester. I'm thankful she patiently helped me cross the finish line.

To my family, I love each of you, though it may not always be obvious.

To Debbie, my wife—we just celebrated forty-two years of marriage, no small accomplishment considering the many challenges we faced. Thank you for never giving up on me or us and for your support as I shared our lives vulnerably in this book. Remember the promise I made to you.

To my children, Matthew, Nicholas, and Morgan—each of you has been uniquely crafted. You are caring and compassionate toward others and bring joy to my heart. I am proud of each of you.

To my mother, Marge, for your love and support. For always being there for me and modeling strength and courage during challenging times. Thank you for preparing me to be a loving son, husband, and father.

To my stepmother, Madeleine, for having the heart of Christ that was in plain sight. Your actions always speak louder than your words. You are a faithful ambassador of God.

To my father, Bill—accepting Jesus' invitation to a new life was your best decision. Though imperfectly lived out, you finished well. I now understand *the* imperfect part better with time. We are all a forgiven work in progress.

To my sisters, Joyce, Lynn, Marge, and Barbara—I love you and cherish my relationship with each of you as your big brother.

To my brothers, Drew and Jim—you are both extraordinary men in my life. But more importantly, thank you for loving my sisters and being great fathers. I love you both.

To Professor Eric Koester and his team at the Creator Institute and Georgetown University for developing an incredible program to help first-time authors get published. Eric, our first conversation changed the direction of this book for the better. Thank you. Thanks to Shanna Heath, head of instruction, for facilitating great conversations every week.

To the team at New Degree Press, thank you for providing a platform to bring my book to life. Special shoutouts to Cassandra Caswell-Stirling, my developmental editor, who got me off to a great start, and to Kenneth W. Cain, my revisions editor, for your patience as we crafted a manuscript worthy of publication. Thanks to Kyra Dawkins for facilitating our weekly meetings. And thanks to John Saunders and Sherman Morrison for your encouragement.

I have been blessed by an incredible extended family, friends, and colleagues, past and present, who have helped shape me into the person I am today. Please accept my heartfelt gratitude for being part of my life.

The following people supported me and believed in the purpose of this book. They offered their time and resources, preordered copies, and helped promote the book before publication. The return on your investment will be countless changed lives. You are all truly amazing. Thank you!

## AMBASSADORS OF HOPE

Debbie Gilmour

Nancy O'Dell

John & Kara Lero

Rick & Laurie Palmen

Phil & Linda Rapp

Slator & Gay Turner

## ENVOYS OF HOPE

Bruce & Karlynn Bucher

Joyce & Drew Kesse

James & Barb White

## ENCOURAGERS OF HOPE

Kristin Carotenuto

Teri Davis

Gary Douglas

Andy Flounders

Claudia Gathman

Margaret Gathman

Daria & Rich Geraffo

Bob & Sue Haines

Josh McClure

Gene Vigil

## IGNITERS OF HOPE

Ralph & Kathy Caprio
Jeanne Carotenuto
Debbie & Chris Caruso
Debbie & Joe Caruso
Greg Gathman
Morgan Gilmour
Brenda Madden

Gayle & John Mattone
Christina & Jeff Miller
Clint Minnicks
Gary & Patty Johnson
Bill & Beth Reichert
Don Ward

## INSPIRERS OF HOPE

Barbara Smith-Dawkins
Graceanne Demcoe
Aidan Ferguson
Denise & Alain Fisher
Kara & Josh Fisher
Mark Harris
Laura & Gilbert Kankowski

Joyce & Drew Kesse
Cathy Massie
Susan & Bill McCarthy
Susan Schmitz
Holly Whitehead
Frank & Carol Zarrillo

## SUPPORTERS OF HOPE

Kyle Albano
Cecilia Ball
Janie Baranyay
Karen Bobrovsky
Paula Brewer
George Chamberlain Sr.
Carolee Christopher
Mary Cisney
Marie Cross
Morgan Davis
Lisa Fahrenkrog
Tracey French
Vincent Gathmann

Cheryl Getkin
Karen Glick
Beverly Guidt
Christopher Lin
Randy Lunn
Vincetta Kane
Amy Kizer
Eric Koester
Cindy Massello
James & Bridget Montesi
Laura Olivieri
Patricia Podkul
Kelly Raymond

Paul & Charisse Ricci  
Suzanne Ritter  
Virginia Ritter  
Linda Sanacore  
Mitch Schrenk

Charles Small  
Katherine Stormer  
Mark Swink  
Sarah Turner  
Vinnie Zarrillo

This book is about *inspiring hope*. Thank you to every individual whose story is shared, as they will make an eternal difference in many lives. Some names have been changed to protect their privacy.

# APPENDIX

## INTRODUCTION

Batterson, Mark. 2013. "The Inverted Gospel." Essay. In *Going All in: One Decision Can Change Everything*, 18. Grand Rapids, MI: Zondervan.

Buxton, Sara. 2020. "Comparative Suffering Is Dangerous." Center Psychotherapy. April 20, 2020. https://center-chicagocbm.com/blog/2020/4/20/comparative-suffering-is-dangerous.

Merriam-Webster. "Hope Definition & Meaning." Merriam-Webster. Accessed November 1, 2022. https://www.merriam-webster.com/dictionary/hope.

Stanley, Andy (@AndyStanley). 2018. "When Somebody Predicts Their Own Death and Resurrection and Pulls It off, We Should Go with Whatever That Person Says. #Reclaimingirresistible." Twitter, October 22, 2018, 2:30 p.m. https://twitter.com/andystanley/status/1054439806577635330.

"Webster's Dictionary 1828 - Hope." Webster's Dictionary 1828. Accessed November 1, 2022. https://webstersdictionary1828.com/Dictionary/hope.

## PART 1

## CHAPTER 1: JENNIFER IS MISSING

Florida Fish and Wildlife Conservation Commission. 2022. "Lakes and Rivers." *Florida Fish and Wildlife Conservation Commission.* Accessed October 6. https://myfwc.com/fishing/freshwater/sites-forecasts/lakes-and-rivers/.

Key West Aquarium, 2022. "Alligator Exhibit at Key West Aquarium." *Key West Aquarium.* September 20. https://www.keywestaquarium.com/ultimate-guide-alligators.

## CHAPTER 2: AN UNRAVELING LIFE

Andrews, Andy. 2009. "Chapter 7." Essay. In *The Noticer - Sometimes, All a Person Needs Is a Little Perspective*, 111. Nashville, TN: Thomas Nelson.

American Psychological Association. 2022. "APA Dictionary of Psychology." *American Psychological Association*. Accessed October 12. https://dictionary.apa.org/self.

Kierkegaard, Søren. 1962. "Part 1 Chapter 1 Loves Hidden Life and Its Recognisability By Its Fruit." Essay. In *Works of Love*, First Harper Torchbook edition published 1964, 23. New York, NY: Harper & Row.

Lewis, C. S. 2011. "God...Shouts in Our Pains." *GOD...SHOUTS IN OUR PAINS*. The Wisdom of C. S. Lewis. June 2. http://cslewiswisdom.blogspot.com/2011/06/godshouts-in-our-pains.html.

Mattone, John. 2020. "Chapter 3 The Vulnerability Decision." Essay. In *The Intelligent Leader: Unlocking the 7 Secrets to Leading Others and Leaving Your Legacy*, 42. Hoboken, NJ: John Wiley & Sons, Inc.

Stanley, Andy. 2008. "Chapter 2 - Why Bad Things Happen to Smart People." Essay. In *The Principle of the Path - How to Get from Where You Are to Where You Want to Be*, 14–15. Nashville, TN: Thomas Nelson.

## PART TWO: INVITATIONS

## CHAPTER 3: AN INVITATION TO CHURCH

Keller, Timothy, and Timothy Keller. 2008. "Epilogue - Where Do We Go from Here?" Essay. In *The Reason for God: Belief in an Age of Skepticism*, First printing, February 2008, 227. New York, NY: Dutton (a member of Penguin Group).

## CHAPTER 4: AN UNEXPECTED INVITATION

Mattone, John. 2020. "Chapter 8 Course Correction." Essay. In *The Intelligent Leader: Unlocking the 7 Secrets to Leading Others and Leaving Your Legacy*, 129. Hoboken, NJ: John Wiley & Sons, Inc.

## CHAPTER 5: INVITATION TO BIBLE STUDY

Calvin, John. 2020. "A John Calvin Eleventary." Edited by Name Barry Kuntze. *Dr. George Grant*. Standfast. May 18. https://georgegrant.net/a-john-calvin-eleventary/.

Gilmour, Bill. 2006. "Making Sense of Jennifer Kesse Tragedy." *Orlando Sentinel*. December 22. https://www.orlandosentinel.com/news/os-xpm-2006-12-22-myword22b-story.html.

Kennedy, Titus. 2018. "The Value of Children in Antiquity." *Drive Thru History Adventures*. March 2. https://drivethruhistoryadventures.com/value-children-antiquity/.

MacArthur, John. 2008. "Table Talk on Trouble and Triumph, Part 1." *Grace to You*. February 17. https://www.gty.org/library/sermons-library/42-270/table-talk-on-trouble-and-triumph-part-1.


## PART THREE: LEARNING TO LISTEN

## CHAPTER 6: LISTENING IS CHALLENGING

Andrews, Andy. 2009. "Chapter 5." Essay. In *The Noticer - Sometimes, All a Person Needs Is a Little Perspective*, 65. Nashville, TN: Thomas Nelson.

Bennett, Roy T. 2011. "Offering a Listening Ear and an Understanding Heart." *The Light in the Heart*. November 14. https://thelightintheheart.wordpress.com/author/roytbennett/page/5/.

Bennett, Roy T. 2019. "Listen with Curiosity." *The Light in the Heart*. August 24. https://thelightintheheart.wordpress.com/2019/08/24/listen-with-curiosity-8/.

Katz, Neil, and Kevin McNulty. 1994. "Reflective Listening." *Maxwell.syr.edu*. https://www.maxwell.syr.edu/docs/default-source/ektron-files/reflective-listening-nk.pdf.

Keller, Tim. 2021. "One of the Main Reasons That We Trust God Too Little Is Because We Trust Our Own Wisdom Too Much. We Think We Know Far Better than God How Our Lives Should Go and What Will Make Us Happy." *Twitter - Tim Keller Wisdom*. @DailyKeller. January 25. https://twitter.com/DailyKeller/status/1353882893337194496.

Goff, Bob. 2022. "Chapter 2 - THE KEYHOLE OF ETERNITY." Essay. In *Undistracted: Capture Your Purpose, Rediscover Your Joy*, 21. Nashville, TN: Nelson Books, an imprint of Thomas Nelson.

Miller, Donald. 2020. "Business Made Simple with Donald Miller: Nir Eyal-The Secret to Staying Focused at Work on Apple Podcasts." *Apple Podcasts*. Business Made Simple. August 31. https://podcasts.apple.com/us/podcast/business-made-simple-with-donald-miller/id1092751338?i=1000489640868.

Price, Catherine. 2018. "Trapped - the Secret Ways Social Media Is Built to Be Addictive (and What You Can Do to Fight Back)." *The Secret Ways Social Media Is Built to Be Addictive | BBC Science Focus Magazine*. BBC Science Focus Magazine. October 29. https://www.sciencefocus.com/future-technology/trapped-the-secret-ways-social-media-is-built-to-be-addictive-and-what-you-can-do-to-fight-back/.

Stanley, Andy. 2018. "Direction, Not Intention, Determines Your Destination. Pic.twitter.com/Opujpxsmrq." *Twitter*. @AndyStanley. September 13. https://twitter.com/andystanley/status/1040306647145566210

## CHAPTER 7: WORDS MATTER

Keller, Timothy. 2022. "Generally Speaking, Fools Think They Are Wise and 100% Right and the Wise Are Aware of the Incompleteness of Their Wisdom and Their Continued Foolishness. Thus the Foolish Call out Everyone and the Wise Do It Sometimes but Realize How Different Things May Look in 5 yrs." *Twitter.* @timkellernyc. September 18.
https://twitter.com/timkellernyc/status/1571470627587907584

Luntz, Frank I. 2007. "Chapter 1 - The Ten Rules of Effective Language." Essay. In *Words That Work: It's Not What You Say, It's What People Hear*, 18. New York, New York: Hyperion.

Mulvaney, Kat. 2020. "Chapter 10 - The New You" Essay. In *A Good Day at School: Take Charge of Emotions so Your Child Can Find Happiness*, Kindle 1194. New York, New York: Morgan James Publishing.

Schwartz, L.C.S.W., Mel. 2019. "Our Words Matter." *Psychology Today.* Sussex Publishers. April 10.
https://www.psychologytoday.com/us/blog/shift-mind/201904/our-words-matter.

Sharma, Robin. 2012. "Words Can Inspire. And Words Can Destroy. Choose Yours Well." *Twitter.* @RobinSharma. September 28.
https://twitter.com/robinsharma/status/251732082957631489.

Warren, Rick. 2002. "Chapter 16 - What Matters Most." Essay. In *The Purpose Driven Life: What on Earth Am I Here for?* 127. Grand Rapids, MN: Zondervan.

Wuerffel, Danny. 2021. "TEDxPaceAcademy." In *The Force of Words.* TEDx Pace Academy.
https://www.youtube.com/watch?v=QwQj2q6-CcE.

## CHAPTER 8: LISTENING SETBACKS

Andrews, Andy. 2009. "Chapter 5." Essay. In *The Noticer - Sometimes, All a Person Needs Is a Little Perspective*, 65. Nashville, TN: Thomas Nelson.

Keller, Tim. 2021. "One of the Main Reasons That We Trust God Too Little Is Because We Trust Our Own Wisdom Too Much. We Think We Know Far Better than God How Our Lives Should Go and What Will Make Us Happy." *Twitter - Tim Keller Wisdom.* @DailyKeller. January 25.
https://twitter.com/DailyKeller/status/1353882893337194496.

Warren, Rick. 2012. "Day 22 – Created to Become Like Christ." Essay. In *Purpose Driven Life - What on Earth Am I Here for?* Expanded Edition (softcover), 174. Grand Rapids, MI: Zondervan.

Warren, Rick. 2002. "Day 25 - Transformed by Trouble." Essay. In *The Purpose Driven Life: What on Earth Am I Here for?* 199. Grand Rapids, MI: Zondervan.

# PART FOUR: FINDING HOPE

## CHAPTER 9: IN THE BIBLE

Chibwe, Chanshi. "10 Surprising Facts about the Bible." The Christian Post. Voices, July 31, 2019. https://www.christianpost.com/voices/10-surprising-facts-the-bible.html.

Miller, William, ed. 1955. "Death of a Genius, His Fourth Dimension, Time, Overtakes Einstein." Google Books. Life Magazine. May 2. https://books.google.com/books?id=dlYEAAAAMBAJ&lpg=PP1&dq=Life%2C+2+May+1955&pg=PA61#v=onepage&q=Life%2C%202%20May%201955&f=false.

Moody, Dwight L, and Dwight L Moody. 2020. "Let Us Pray - Prayer Guide." *Www.moodycenter.org.* Moody Center. May 26. https://moodycenter.org/wp-content/uploads/2020/05/Prayer-Guide_052620.pdf.

Stanley, Andy. 2014. "Chapter 1: Start." Essay. In *Starting Point: A Conversation about Faith*, 18. Grand Rapids, MI: Zondervan.

Yancey, Philip Author. 1999. Essay. In *The Bible Jesus Read*, 11. Grand Rapids, MI: Zondervan.

Yancey, Philip Author. 1999. Essay. In *The Bible Jesus Read*, 12. Grand Rapids, MI: Zondervan

Yancey, Philip Author. 1999. Essay. In *The Bible Jesus Read*, 13-14. Grand Rapids, MI: Zondervan

Yancey, Philip Author. 1999. Essay. In *The Bible Jesus Read*, 14. Grand Rapids, MI: Zondervan

Yancey, Philip. 1990. "Chapter 17 - Hope." Essay. In *Where Is God When It Hurts?* 217. Grand Rapids, MI: Zondervan.

## CHAPTER 10: IN A PENDANT

Bright, Bill. 1997. "Chapter 2 - Fasting Transforms Us to Transform the World." Essay. In *The Transforming Power of Fasting and Prayer: Personal Accounts of Spiritual Renewal*, 25. Orlando, FL: NewLife Publications.

Eldredge, John. 2009. "Missing the Most Important Thing — September 6." Essay. In *Knowing the Heart of God: A Year of Daily Readings to Help You Abide in Him*, 249. Nashville, TN: Thomas Nelson.

Link, Rachael. 2018. "8 Health Benefits of Fasting, Backed by Science." *Healthline Nutrition.* Healthline Media. July 30. https://www.healthline.com/nutrition/fasting-benefits.

Piper, John, and Lillian Kwon. 2012. "John Piper Reflects on 30-Year Ministry: Warns Pastors to Avoid Stereotypes." *The Christian Post*. CP Church & Ministries. December 11.
https://www.christianpost.com/news/john-piper-reflects-on-30-year-ministry-warns-pastors-to-avoid-stereotypes.html.

## CHAPTER 11: DURING WAR

Andrews, Andy. 2020. "'Discipline Is the Ability to Make Yourself Do Something You Don't Want to Do in Order to Get a Result You Really Want to Get." — Andy Andrews Pic.twitter.com/9a3fyfs5kd." *Twitter*. @AndyAndrews. June 5.
https://twitter.com/AndyAndrews/status/1268929332241711104.

Baker, James. 2020. "The Five P's: 'Proper Preparation Prevents Poor Performance.'" *HQnotes*. Howe Q. Wallace. October 22.
https://www.hqnotes.com/the-five-ps-proper-preparation-prevents-poor-performance/.

Chance, Todd. 2013. "'What Would You Do?' Host/Reporter John Quinones to Speak at Devos Place." *Mlive.com*. What Would You Do?' host/reporter John Quinones to speak at DeVos Place. October 28.
https://www.mlive.com/entertainment/grand-rapids/2013/10/what_would_you_do_hostreporter.html.

Frost, Natasha. 2021. "Why Stalin Tried to Stamp Out Religion in the Soviet Union." *History.com*. A&E Television Networks. April 23.
https://www.history.com/news/joseph-stalin-religion-atheism-ussr#.

History.com Editors. 2018. "Gulag." *History.com*. A&E Television Networks. March 23.
https://www.history.com/topics/russia/gulag.

Miller, Donald. n.d. "Donald Miller on Productivity 2020." In *Donald Miller Teaches Productivity*, 4. Nashville.

"Tear Down This Wall." 2021.*The Ronald Reagan Presidential Foundation & Institute*. July 21.
https://www.reaganfoundation.org/programs-events/webcasts-and-podcasts/podcasts/a-reagan-forum/tear-down-this-wall/.

Tapalaga, Andrei, and Emily Johnson. 2022. "Letters Depicting the Horrors Lived by Prisoners inside Soviet Gulags." *History of Yesterday*. September 3.
https://historyofyesterday.com/letters-depicting-the-horrors-lived-by-prisoners-inside-soviet-gulags/.

## CHAPTER 12: AFTER IDENTITY CRISIS

Keller, Tim. 2015. "'If Our Identity Is in Our Work, Rather than Christ, Success Will Go to Our Heads, and Failure Will Go to Our Hearts.'." *Twitter*. @DailyKeller. April 16.
https://twitter.com/dailykeller/status/588737464107462656.

Morgan, Kate. 2021. "Why We Define Ourselves by Our Jobs." *BBC Worklife.* BBC. April 13. https://www.bbc.com/worklife/article/20210409-why-we-define-ourselves-by-our-jobs

Rae, Skylar. 2021. "The Two Sides of Your Ego and How to Balance Them." Weblog. *Medium.* July 22. https://skylarrae.medium.com/the-two-sides-of-your-ego-and-how-to-balance-them-810df0442a93.

## CHAPTER 13: AFTER DRIFTING THROUGH LIFE

"About Us: Charity: Water." 2022. *Charity Water.* Accessed September 23. https://www.charitywater.org/about.

Assisi, Saint Francis of, and Father Ed Dougherty. 2021. "Doing the Impossible." *Catholic Review.* March 4. https://catholicreview.org/doing-the-impossible/.

Harrison, Scott. 2017. "The Charity Water Story | Scott Harrison." *YouTube -The Charity Water Story | Scott Harrison.* North Point Community Church. July 26. https://www.youtube.com/watch?v=w8QdFdtsmbs.

"Mission." 2022. *Mercy Ships.* Accessed September 23. https://www.mercyships.org/who-we-are/our-mission/.

Stanley, Andy. 2013. "'In Light of Your Past Experience, Your Current Circumstances, and Your Future Hopes and Dreams, What Is the Wise Thing for You to Do?'." Twitter. @QuotingAndy. November 8. https://twitter.com/quotingandy/status/398903610387759104

## CHAPTER 14: AFTER BROKENNESS

Lewis, Robert. 2003. "Welcome to the Quest." Essay. In *The Quest for Authentic Manhood,* Fourth Printing, 5. Nashville, TN: LifeWay Press.

Stevenson, Bryan. 2015. "Chapter Fifteen - Broken." Essay. In *Just Mercy: A Story of Justice and Redemption,* 2015 Trade Paperback Edition, 290-291. New York, NY: One World (Random House).

## CHAPTER 15: AFTER PRISON

Bullock, Marcus. 2021. "I Was a Teenage Felon S2E9: Marcus Bullock (Super Predator; Vice TV)." *YouTube.* VICE TV. December 29. https://www.youtube.com/watch?v=xDVX5B8DOVA.

Bullock, Marcus. 2019. "An App That Helps Incarcerated People Stay Connected to Their Families." *Marcus Bullock: An App That Helps Incarcerated People Stay Connected to Their Families | TED Talk.* TED Salon. June. https://www.ted.com/talks/marcus_bullock_an_app_that_helps_incarcerated_people_stay_connected_to_their_families.

Bullock, Marcus. 2020. "Marcus Bullock Flikshop Full Episode." Edited by Daniel Kihanya. *YouTube*. Founders Unfound (foundersunfound.com/listento). May 14.
https://www.youtube.com/watch?v=xNxnlDLQxeI.

Edison, Thomas. 1997. "Thomas Edison 'Quotes.'" Edited by Gerald Beals. *Edison Quotes*. ThomasEdison.com. February 11.
https://www.thomasedison.com/quotes.html.

Flikshop School of Business. 2022. "Entrepreneurship-Based Development Program for Emerging Adults." *Flikshopschoolofbusiness*. Accessed October 22.
https://www.flikshopschoolofbusiness.com/.

Flikshop. 2022. "Flikshop Website About Us." *Flikshop*. Accessed October 22.
https://www.flikshop.com/about-us.

Stanley, Andy. 2008. "Chapter 2 - Why Bad Things Happen to Smart People." Essay. In *The Principle of the Path - How to Get from Where You Are to Where You Want to Be*, 14–15. Nashville, TN: Thomas Nelson.

Stevenson, Bryan. 2015. "Chapter Fifteen - Broken." Essay. In *Just Mercy: A Story of Justice and Redemption*, 2015 Trade Paperback Edition, 290–291. New York, NY: One World (Random House).

## CHAPTER 16: AFTER SUICIDE

Beck, Barbara, dir. 2013. "Coping With Grief - Jimmy & Linda Knott GC041813." Broadcast. *The Good Life*. FL, April 18, 2013: Lake Mary.

Boom, Corrie ten, Elizabeth Sherrill, and John Sherrill. 2015. "Chapter 14 The Blue Sweater." Essay. In *The Hiding Place*, eBook, Location 1926. Bloomington, MN: Chosen Books.

CDC, MMWR Supplements. 2022. "Mental Health, Suicidality, and Connectedness among High School Students during the COVID-19 Pandemic - Adolescent Behaviors and Experiences Survey, United States, January–June 2021." *Centers for Disease Control and Prevention*. Centers for Disease Control and Prevention. March 31.
https://www.cdc.gov/mmwr/volumes/71/su/su7103a3.htm.

CDC. 2022. "Facts about Suicide." *Centers for Disease Control and Prevention*. Centers for Disease Control and Prevention. July 25.
https://www.cdc.gov/suicide/facts/index.html#.

First Baptist Church - Orlando, dir. 2015. *What's Your Word? YouTube*. First Orlando.
https://www.youtube.com/watch?v=xonqNyN17Js.

Williams, Litsa. 2014. "Grief and Faith: The Relationship between Grief and Belief." *What's Your Grief?* June 30.
https://whatsyourgrief.com/grief-and-faith-grief-belief/.

## PART FIVE: FAITH IN ACTION

## CHAPTER 17: DONATING LIFE

Andrews, Andy. 2009. "Chapter 5." Essay. In *The Noticer - Sometimes, All a Person Needs Is a Little Perspective*, 8. Nashville, TN: Thomas Nelson.

Lewis, C. S. 1940. "Human Pain." Essay. In *The Problem of Pain*, Softcover91 ed., 91. New York, NY: HarperOne.

Lucado, Max. 2021. "30 Inspirational Max Lucado Quotes to Encourage You Today." Edited by Tessa Emily Hall. *Crosswalk.com*. Crosswalk.com. April 20. https://www.crosswalk.com/faith/spiritual-life/inspirational-max-lucado-quotes-to-encourage-you-today.html.

Stanley, Andy. 2019. "Do for One What You Wish You Could Do for Everyone. Pic.twitter.com/orvpbont4h." *Twitter*. @AndyStanley. March 11. https://twitter.com/andystanley/status/1105084218101641217

## CHAPTER 18: WALKING INTO SPIRITUAL HEALTH

Blackaby, Henry, Richard Blackaby, and Claude King. 2008. "Introduction." Essay. In *Experiencing God, Knowing and Doing the Will of God*, Revised and Expanded, 7. Nashville, TN: B&H Publishing Group.

Keller, Timothy. 2017. "Jesus Didn't Come to Tell Us the Answers to the Questions of Life, He Came to Be the Answer." *Twitter*. @timkellernyc. October 5. https://twitter.com/timkellernyc/status/915940683701264385

Stanley, Charles F. 2002. "Chapter 10 - Listen & Obey." Essay. In *How to Listen to God*, eBook, 135.

Stanley, Charles F. 2005. "Principle 5 - Obedience Always Brings Blessings." Essay. In *Living the Extraordinary Life Nine Principles to Discover It*, 85. Nashville, TN: Thomas Nelson. Nashville, TN: Thomas Nelson.

Warren, Rick. 2012. "Day 37 - Sharing Your Message." Essay. In *The Purpose Driven Life - What on Earth Am I Here For?* Expanded Edition, 288. Grand Rapids, Michigan: Zondervan.

## PART SIX: CALL TO ACTION

## CHAPTER 19: SEEK IDENTITY AND PURPOSE

Stanley, Andy. 2013. "'In Light of Your Past Experience, Your Current Circumstances, and Your Future Hopes and Dreams, What Is the Wise Thing for You to Do?'" Twitter. @QuotingAndy. November 8. https://twitter.com/quotingandy/status/398903610387759104.

Warren, Rick. 2002. "Contents." Essay. In *The Purpose Driven Life: What on Earth Am I Here for?* Grand Rapids, MI: Zondervan.

Warren, Rick. 2002. "Day 5 – Seeing Life from God's View." Essay. In *The Purpose Driven Life - What on Earth Am I Here For?* 42. Grand Rapids, Michigan: Zondervan.

Warren, Rick. 2002. "Day 11 – Becoming Best Friends with God." Essay. In *The Purpose Driven Life - What on Earth Am I Here For?* 85–86. Grand Rapids, Michigan: Zondervan.

Warren, Rick. 2002. "Day 11 – Seeing Life from God's View." Essay. In *The Purpose Driven Life - What on Earth Am I Here For?* 91. Grand Rapids, Michigan: Zondervan.

Warren, Rick. 2002. "Day 14 – When God Seems Distant." Essay. In *The Purpose Driven Life - What on Earth Am I Here For?* 109. Grand Rapids, Michigan: Zondervan.

Warren, Rick. 2012. "Day 1 – It All Starts with God." Essay. In *The Purpose Driven Life - What on Earth Am I Here For?* Expanded Edition, 21. Grand Rapids, Michigan: Zondervan.

## CHAPTER 20: SEVENTEEN YEARS LATER

King, Jr., Martin Luther. 2022. "Martin Luther King, Jr. Memorial Quotations - South Wall." *National Parks Service.* US Department of the Interior. Accessed October 27.
https://www.nps.gov/mlkm/learn/quotations.htm.

Made in the USA
Middletown, DE
14 April 2024